—

Making It Home

The Story of Catharine Parr Traill

Making It Home

The Story of Catharine Parr Traill

by

Lynn Westerhout

Illustrations by Liz Milkau

Series Editor: Allister Thompson

Napoleon Publishing

Napoleon Publishing
Toronto Ontario Canada

Napoleon Publishing acknowledges
the support of the Canada Council for the Arts
for our publishing program.

Le Conseil des Arts | The Canada Council
du Canada | for the Arts

Printed in Canada

Library and Archives Canada Cataloguing in Publication

Westerhout, Lynn, date-
    Making it home : the story of Catharine Parr Traill / Lynn Westerhout.

ISBN 0-929141-90-3

    1. Traill, Catherine Parr, 1802-1899--Juvenile literature. 2. Frontier and pioneer life-
-Ontario--Juvenile literature.   3. Women pioneers--Ontario--Biography--Juvenile literature.
4. Women authors, Canadian (English)--19th century--Biography--Juvenile literature.
5. Women authors, Canadian (English)--Ontario--Biography--Juvenile literature. I. Title.

PS8439.T7Z93 2004 j971.3'02'092   C2004-903225-9

I dedicate this book to my mother,
Betty Irene Clifford Westerhout,
whose favourite flower
is the rose baywillow herb.

Catharine Parr Traill: Natural Storyteller

Catharine Parr Traill loved to write. She wrote stories in secret as a child, knowing she would be punished if she were caught. As an adult, she wrote while she was hungry and fearful for the safety of her own babies. She even wrote when it hurt to hold the pen.

Her work and her life were pioneering. Her stories for children were part of a new focus on young people. Her books on emigration encouraged other pioneers who struggled with life in a new country. She was one of the first to record the Ontario wilderness in literary and scientific detail.

Catharine wrote for herself, her family and for the public. She wrote to earn money, but her work showed that wonder, courage and faith are most important in life. These ideas were vital to her, but what in her own life shaped these beliefs and her writing? How did an English girl called Katie, born way before computers, typewriters or even fountain pens were invented, grow up to give so much to Canada's early literature?

Katie

Catharine began life with a story. Born January 9, 1802 in England, she was named after historic Queen Catherine Parr, a distant relative of her father. Young Catharine was known in the family as "The Katie", as if she were royalty too!

She was the fifth daughter of Thomas Strickland and his wife Elizabeth Homer. Her older sisters were Eliza, Agnes, Sarah and Jane. Blue-eyed Katie was the pet of them all. A year later, her younger sister Susanna was born, and then two brothers, Samuel and Thomas.

London in the 19th century

Catharine's father made money managing the shipping docks at Rotherhithe, near the capital city of London. The family ate good food and wore fashionable clothes. They could afford luxuries such as books and servants to do the house and garden work.

Queen Catherine Parr

NAMESAKES AND NICKNAMES

Queen Catherine Parr was the sixth and last wife of King Henry the Eighth of England. She lived from 1512 to 1548. Katie is a short form of Catharine. Eliza is short for Elizabeth, and Susanna was often called Susie. When Catharine's brother Thomas was a baby, he tried to say Sarah, and it came out "Thay". Soon all the family called her that.

First Garden

Catharine was a year old when doctors told her father to stop working so hard and move to the country. The family rented Stowe House, near the town of Bungay, Suffolk, in the valley of the Waveney River.

There were farms all around and a garden. A tiny stream trickled through a wild area behind some hedges. In spring, violets and primroses flowered, and Catharine and her sisters played for hours under the honeysuckle branches. They drank stream water from acorn cups and made flower beds fenced with little stones. Catharine begged plant roots and bulbs from the chief gardener and found an old tin teapot for a watering can.

Society was divided into classes. Families belonged to a class, depending on how much money they had and how it was earned. Most families believed each should keep to their place in society. Families whose ancestors had been lords and ladies would rarely mix with businessmen's families. Businessmen's children did not play with servants' or farmworkers' children.

She sat and listened while her big sister Eliza sang long dramatic ballads. She imagined magical creatures in the ivy when Jane told fairy stories. She called it "our Eden", thinking of the perfect garden in the Bible story. Her parents often read aloud from this book of historical and miraculous tales, the basis for the religions of Judaism and Christianity.

A Favourite In the Family

Catharine faced the world with a gentle, inner calm, like her sister Sarah, who shared her bed and bedroom. Describing "the Katie" when she was little, Sarah said she didn't cry like other children. Tears just rolled quietly down her cheeks, "like pearls".

Catharine made peace when her sisters argued. She disliked making bossy Eliza or haughty Agnes angry. She preferred to get on with life rather than fuss, so she never held a grudge if she had been wronged.

She played mostly with Susanna. Catharine loved her wild, romantic imagination, "tinged with gloom and grandeur".

There was also a special bond between Catharine and her father. She was curious to know all he could teach her. She did not get bored or tired easily when they went out walking in the woods or fishing.

Her father had a painful joint disease called gout. Catharine was instinctively sympathetic to those who suffered, physically or emotionally. She learned to be helpful when he had to stay in bed and cheer him with stories of her daily activities.

Agnes Strickland, Susanna and Catharine's sister

Susanna Strickland

Home Schooling

KATIE'S MEMORY

Seventy years later, she could still remember the first verse of a book called *History of the Reformation in Rhyme* by Ward.

I sing the deeds of good King Harry
And Ned his son and daughter Mary
And of a short-lived interreign
Of one fair queen hight Lady Jane.

Maybe the poem stuck in Catharine's mind because it was about the period in history when Queen Catherine Parr lived. At one time the book was banned and all copies ordered to be burned. Different rulers have tried to control people's thinking and beliefs by doing this.

Catharine's brothers went to school in the nearby city of Norwich to prepare for a career. The girls stayed home, learning to sew clothes and curtains, cook, and make butter and cheese. These household skills suited the only job they were expected to have—wife. Catharine's mother hoped her daughter would marry a rich man and only need to supervise servants.

But her parents were unusual for their time. They thought girls should also learn academic subjects.

Catharine learned to read from her mother. She read the books in her father's library; atlases describing far away lands and essays on many subjects. Her father taught her geography, history and math. She learned some French and Latin. She had lessons in drawing and watercolour painting, but Catharine did poorly in art.

She easily memorized poetry. When the children acted Shakespeare's play *The Tempest* for fun, Catharine took the role of Ariel, a magical spirit trying to win back his freedom.

Outdoor Education

THRUSHES' ANVIL

A thrush is a brown songbird that likes to eat snails. When captured, the snails curl up in their shells to escape, but the thrush will lay them on a flat stone and hammer them with its sharp beak until the shell cracks. Other birds use similar ways to get at shelled animals. Gulls will fly up and drop clams onto a rock to break them.

Bungay Castle

Catharine loved learning natural history and biology best. Her father taught her the names of trees and flowers, how to recognize birds by their songs, why a certain stone was covered with broken snail shells as they fished or strolled. Nothing was too small to be noticed or wondered about, even spiders, which Catharine admired but never liked.

She began collecting; hazelnut shells like pig noses, bright orange fungi on rotting wood, patterned stones, anything that seemed special was carried home in a basket.

Catharine and her mother decided which was the discovery of the day, the "pearl". It was placed on the schoolroom shelf. The rest, the "pebbles", decorated her bedroom windowsill until spring cleaning time.

Sometimes Catharine walked to Bungay's ruined castle or went in the carriage to the town market. The work of harness makers, potters and coopers, who made barrels, sparked her imagination. As the horses trotted home, Catharine imagined what she would write for her composition lesson the next day.

Moving to Reydon Hall

Reydon Hall

MARTIN'S POEM

In a cottage we will live
Happy, though of low estate
Every hour more bliss will bring
We in goodness shall be great.

M. E.

The Stricklands moved house again on Christmas Eve, 1808. Catharine, nearly seven, travelled with her big sisters in an open cart. The bitter wind blew from the nearby sea. She was cold, even though double-wrapped in Eliza's velvet pelisse, a kind of dress coat, and a heavy greatcoat. They stopped at a place called Deadman's Grave to buy straw to keep their feet warm.

Their new home, Reydon Hall, stood outside Reydon village. Shivering, they explored huge reception rooms, many bedrooms and attics full of cobwebs, dust and broken furniture.

The servants told the girls there were two ghosts haunting the place! An old woman in grey was supposed to play such bad tricks that your hair turned white overnight. An old man named Martin had lived in the attic and left a poem scratched on a window pane. Catharine did not admit she was scared, but she never forgot Martin's poem.

7

This fossil is called a trilobite

FAMOUS FOSSIL HUNTER

Another girl, about the same age as Catharine, was also hunting fossils at this time.

Mary Anning (1799-1847) found the first complete Icthyosaur fossil, in 1810, when she was aged eleven. She continued her work as she grew up and later discovered two complete Plesiosaurs and the first Pteradactyl found in Britain. Her work was extremely important for the new scientific ideas that Charles Darwin summed up in his book *On The Origin of Species*, published in 1859.

Wider Outdoors

Catharine's little Eden had been left behind, but she enjoyed the surroundings of Reydon Hall. She read in the shade of the huge sycamore tree in the middle of the lawn, or strolled in the grove of oaks. She explored Reydon Woods, looking for bluebells. Out in the countryside with her sisters, she visited local historic sites.

Best of all, there was the beach. Trudging the sands, Catharine scanned the tideline pebbles for agate, amber or carnelian, semi-precious stones she could have tumbled and polished in the nearby town of Southwold.

Sometimes she found strange impressions in the rocks, snail shells and beetle-like creatures. Were these really the remains of animals that lived long ago? Could this be evidence of the new idea that the world was hundreds of thousands of years old? Like most people in Europe, Catharine knew the story of the beginning of world as told in the Bible. Would she have to choose which to believe? Was there a story that could account for it all? Catharine was always curious.

NEW LITERATURE

Novels were becoming popular. At first they were thought to be acceptable if they were written by a man, such as Sir Walter Scott. Some women published theirs under men's names, like Mary Ann Evans, who wrote as George Eliot. Others, like Fanny Burney or Jane Austen, did use their own names, but they risked the anger of their families and a loss of status in the eyes of other members of their social class. That is, until they became best sellers and were recognized by the royal family!

Jane Austen

George Eliot

Catharine Breaks the Rules

Catharine's parents held strict views about behaviour. Young ladies of her time were not supposed to scramble and romp. When she stayed out too late, got mud on her pinafore or tore her muslin dress climbing, Catharine offered her mother wild strawberries threaded on a grass stem to soften her anger. It didn't always work. She still might have to spend time alone in her room, be forbidden to go outside or miss dessert in the dining room for three days.

Rules existed about what to write and read. Catharine could learn poetry about grand subjects by great authors but not make it up herself. Information books, or books with morals that showed how to behave were all that she was supposed to read. Adventure novels were forbidden—unless her father read them aloud. Likely he pointed out the morals as he told the story.

Catharine rarely suffered her father's anger, because she did not argue about these rules. She did not wish to upset him. Instead she wrote poems and read some books secretly.

Caught In the Act

Young Catharine

WRITING MATERIALS

Pens were made of goose feathers, with the shaft trimmed at a square angle. They were dipped in ink made from lampblack (soot—carbon particles) and water.

Paper was made from pulped vegetable matter such as flax or hemp, or from cotton rags. It was not made in the quantities we see today, as the processes for using wood pulp and big powered rolling mills had not yet been perfected. It came in large uncut sheets, and in different colours.

Catharine sometimes stayed at Reydon in Eliza's care while her parents visited her brothers at school in Norwich. Once, she and Susanna wanted to amuse themselves writing stories, rules or not. In a papier mâché chest once owned by a prince from India, underneath embroidered silk, they found paper and cut quill pens. Taking ink, each girl started writing an adventure. They read them to Sarah in secret.

Catharine's was about a boy, his pet marmot and the Swiss Revolution. Her plot got so tangled she had to stop. She began a story for young children instead.

Then Catharine's mother returned unexpectedly and caught them! She didn't say much, but her older sister Eliza harshly criticized girls who wasted their time with such trash. She upset Susanna, who threw her papers on the fire.

Catharine promised to cut her pages up and use them to wrap her hair in curls at night. But she destroyed only a few pages and hid the rest. "Scribbling fever", as she and Susanna called it, had taken strong hold and would last the rest of their lives.

A typical English river

A Big Change

In 1818, when she was sixteen, Catharine's father loaned someone a large amount of money. When it was not repaid, the family became much poorer. Thomas Strickland, already ill, had a heart attack and died.

Catharine had known death in the family before. There was a baby sister, Eleanor, who had died when Catharine was nine, but her father was the most important person in her life. She grieved deeply, walking often to his grave to place fresh flowers.

In order to appear respectable and keep their place in society, Catharine's mother did not sell Reydon Hall. She closed most of it up. The unused rooms smelled of damp and rats, but Mrs. Strickland continued to live there with Sarah, Jane and Susanna. To afford this, the girls had to do a lot of the house and garden work, and the carriage and horses were sold.

The Norwich house was kept too, as Samuel, thirteen, and Thomas, eleven, still went to school. Catharine, Agnes and Eliza lived there with the boys during school terms.

BURIAL PLACE

Thomas Strickland was staying in Norwich, close to his business partners and doctor. Catharine and her two eldest sisters were with him. He died two days before he was due to return to the rest of the family at Reydon Hall. He was buried in the churchyard in Lakenham, near Norwich, so that he could still be in the countryside he loved.

LIFELONG TREASURE

Grown-up Catharine's favourite possession was a book she had loved since she was seven. It had belonged to her father, and it was a first edition copy of *The Compleat Angler* by Izaak Walton, published in 1653. (No, the title is not spelled wrong; spelling rules were different then.)

Walton wrote about the joys of fishing and country life. Catharine thought it helped form her love of nature. Walton also wrote biographies of famous poets.

What Could the Future Hold?

Catharine found her sixteenth year very hard. Her father, her special companion, was dead. She was separated from Susanna, and she was under the control of Eliza and Agnes, now in their twenties.

Catharine went to few social activities. The year after a parent's death was expected to be passed quietly. She found comfort in walks to a garden outside the city, and she read for hours, mulling over ideas she found in books borrowed from the library.

As the sisters went about their daily chores, lively discussions ensued. Was slavery right or wrong? What sort of government was best? How should a person who believed in God show those beliefs? Should women have more rights to decide their own lives?

And more particularly, how could Catharine, Eliza and Agnes be independent without money of their own? Upper middle class women did not become shopkeepers, seamstresses, governesses or servants unless they were desperate. If the Strickland girls did not marry well, the future held only a life restricted by poverty. There were few other choices.

CATHARINE'S WAY OUT

Though she'd said scribbling was a waste of time, eventually Eliza became editor of the *Court Journal* in London.

Agnes first published poetry, but it did not sell well. She became famous for writing the *Lives of the Queens of England*, with Eliza. Jane wrote for the annuals, a mix of short stories and poems that publishers produced yearly. Susanna wrote essays and poetry for magazines.

Catharine's brothers each wrote a book about their lives. Sarah was the only Strickland sibling who never appeared in print. "Thay's" claim to fame was as the best baker in the family!

A Writer Is Discovered

Lonely Catharine turned to writing again. Her imagination soared when she heard the wailing pipes of the Scottish shepherds, come down from the Highlands to sell their sheep in town. Familiar with Scottish history, she wrote "The Blind Highland Piper". Delivery boys with buckets on yokes over their shoulders inspired "The Little Water Carrier".

Outside picking red currants one day, Catharine suddenly remembered she'd left her stories uncovered on the desk. She hurried in. The manuscript was gone. Dreading a fight with Eliza, Catharine said nothing, but soon all secrets were out.

Mr. Morgan, their legal guardian, had come to sign papers for Eliza, who was now the family's money manager. While waiting for her, Mr. Morgan had discovered Catharine's stories and assumed they were Eliza's. She was astonished when he came back with amazing news. A publisher in London would pay five guineas, gold coins, to make a book of "The Blind Highland Piper" and other stories. Eliza could not be angry with Catharine now. This was the first money the Strickland girls had ever earned other than pennies for gardening as small children.

TEACHING YOUNG NATURE LOVERS

Catharine published four other wildlife books in this period. *Sketches from Nature; or Hints to Juvenile Naturalists* came out in 1830. She spent part of the money from *Sketches* on a pony named Pedro to pull the cart at Reydon Hall. Catharine decided he was a bad bargain because he was "balky", and stubborn, but she blamed her own mismanagement of him for some of his bad temper.

Sketchbook of a Young Naturalist; or Hints to the Students of Nature, Narratives of Nature, and *History Book for Young Naturalists* all came out in 1831.

Writing a Book a Year

Catharine worked steadily through her twenties as a writer of stories for children. She thought that stories should teach as well as amuse. This is shown in her two-part titles, such as "The Keepsake Guineas; or The Best Use of Money" and "Prejudice Reproved; or The History of the Negro Toyseller". Her characters were rewarded or punished depending on their actions.

Catharine's most successful stories drew on her knowledge of nature. For "Little Downy; the History of a Field Mouse", she watched the movements of a real mouse living near an oak tree, took notes on a chalk slate, then hurried home to rewrite them.

Her nature theme was strong in the little stories and poems she wrote for publisher's annuals, collections that usually came out just before Christmas. Her own collection of original nursery rhymes was titled *The Flower Basket; or Poetical Blossoms.*

When her brother Sam emigrated to Canada, the wilderness he described in letters home made a strong impression on her, and she wrote *The Young Emigrants; or Pictures of Life in Canada*, published in 1826.

London and First Love

Thomas Pringle

POET AND REFORMER

Thomas Pringle (1789-1834) was a Scottish editor and poet. He led the Anti-Slavery League, and Catharine and Susanna attended meetings and discussions. Susanna wrote down the experiences of two former slaves. These were published and used as part of the argument to get the British Parliament to abolish slavery.

Pringle edited *Athenaeum* magazine and *Friendship's Offering*, which Catharine wrote for. Catharine first met Thomas Traill at the Pringle house. Later Catharine was friends with Pringle relatives who emigrated to Gore's Landing, Upper Canada.

Catharine made too little money to live by herself. She helped with expenses at Reydon Hall and visited London, where Agnes, Eliza and Susanna now lived. She met other writers such as poet Thomas Pringle.

At twenty-seven, Catharine found romance at home. She became engaged to marry Francis Harral, a medical student, son of the editor of a women's fashion magazine, *La Belle Assemblée.* But the Harrals moved with Francis to London.

This separation hurt. She wrote to the poet James Bird and his wife Emma: "I must see Francis since he is unable to come to me... I am and can be very firm upon occasions... They do not know how determined Katie can be when the welfare of those she loves are at all concerned."

Francis' stepmother disliked Catharine, and he did not stop her embarassing Catharine by putting announcements about her private life in the newspapers.

Heartbroken, Catharine ended their engagement to spare both him and herself further torment. At the same time, Susanna decided to marry John Dunbar Moodie. Catharine tried not to let her own sadness spoil her sister's joy.

Travel Cures the Blues

NO WOMEN ALLOWED

At this time, Catharine only enjoyed Oxford University's appearance. She would not have been able to study there. The first hall for women was opened in 1878, but they were not allowed to be full university members until 1920.

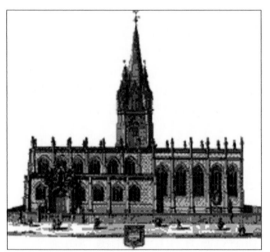

Oxford University in the 19th century

Catharine was the only family member to attend her sister's wedding, a quiet celebration held in London. She was so depressed and ill afterward that she was unable even to write.

Her wealthy older cousin, Rebecca Leverton, took Catharine to stay at her country estate. There she roamed the gardens and spent time in the dairy. She visited schools set up by the Levertons for poor children and helped to teach. The students loved her. Rebecca then took her to the city of Bath and to Oxford, whose ancient university buildings she admired. Gradually, she felt better.

She returned to London briefly before going back to Reydon Hall at the beginning of 1832. Two pieces of news made it urgent that she be there, close to Southwold, where Susanna and her new husband, John Moodie, were living.

One was that a baby was expected in February. Catharine would become an aunt for the first time.

The other was that the Moodies were planning to go and live in Canada.

16

Canada Mania

Settlers dreamed of owning big estates like this one, painted by Anne Langton, who came to live in Canada in 1837.

Catharine understood why the Moodies thought of such a drastic move. Thousands of people, hungry for a better future, listened to William Cattermole, from Bungay. He worked for the land sale companies. He, and others like him, told wonderful stories of how a pioneer could be rich after only a few years.

Robert Reid, from Upper Canada, father of their brother Sam's wife and a successful settler himself, visited the Moodies and encouraged them.

Catharine knew she might never see Susanna again. The distance was great and travel very expensive. There were hazards; disease, accident, weather, crime.

To make the most of the last few months, she stayed at Reydon Hall and visited Susanna every day. She cuddled her first niece, named Catherine, and listened to lively John talk about the future. She calmed her nervous and imaginative sister, helping her to see the benefits of going, helping her decide what to take with her.

And every day at her brother-in-law's house, she met a quiet, studious friend of his, Thomas Traill.

JOHN MOODIE

Susanna's husband was an officer in an army that now needed few officers. He was the youngest son of an aristocratic family, who had no money and no hope of inheriting any land. He was educated, adventurous and desperate to find a way to make a secure living. He farmed in South Africa for a while, but Susanna did not want to go back there with him.

Catharine's Husband

WEDDING

Catharine's engagement was angrily opposed by her mother and her other sisters. They wanted "The Katie" to be wealthy and within reach of visits. But Catharine was determined. This time, no one would prevent her marriage.

Eventually, Agnes and Jane agreed to be bridesmaids. Even her mother, who hated to leave home, attended Reydon's Church of St. Margaret on May 13, 1832. John Moodie led Catharine down the aisle to Thomas. Taking his hand, Katie Strickland became Catharine Parr Traill.

She wrote she was "willing to lose all for the sake of one dear valued friend and husband."

Thomas Traill was a tall, thin Scot from the Orkney Islands. He had served in the army with Moodie during the Napoleonic wars, in the Royal Northern Fusiliers. He was widowed, with two teenage sons. He was on half-pay service, though it was unlikely he would be called back to duty. Like Moodie, he was now too poor to live in the old, aristocratic way. He had travelled in Europe and loved reading and languages. He very much respected Catharine's writing.

Catharine was only thirty, while he was thirty-nine. Their love was a deep but quiet affair. She knew he needed her, like her father and Susanna, to be an anchor in his life, to balance the fears and sadness that came to him so easily. Thomas was inspired by her spirit, so much so that the gentle professor was even willing to try chopping wood in the wilderness with her.

Newlyweds Catharine and Thomas would emigrate to Canada too.

First To Scotland

TRAILL'S HOME

The Orkneys are an archipelago of sixty-seven low, treeless, windswept islands, off the northeast coast of Scotland. The weather would be very cold if not for the Gulf Stream, which moderates the temperature enough for farming. Thomas Traill's estate of Westove was near Kirkwall, the main town on the biggest island.

Catharine said heartwrenching goodbyes to her family. She knew there was little chance she would see her mother again or read to sweet Sarah. Even her plans to meet Susanna at Sam's in Canada could fail. But she set her face to the future and focussed on the impressive scenery of Scotland.

Thomas' family gave her a warm welcome. His cousins thought of her as "lovely, bright, and sunny". They were disappointed she was not to stay, although they understood why. Times were hard for them too.

She met Thomas's sons, Walter, seventeen, and John, thirteen. Neither of them was interested in going to Canada. They were well settled with Barbara Fotheringhame, their mother's sister. Once more, sad farewells were spoken.

Catharine and Thomas travelled to the port of Greenock, outside of Glasgow. Here they bought ship passage, tickets for a brig called the *Rowley,* which set sail for Canada the first week of July 1832.

Ill Start

Just before they left, Catharine took sick, but the journey could not wait. Crossing the Atlantic took at least six weeks, and they had to arrive well before winter. Good passage was hard to find. They paid a lot to be on a cargo boat with few passengers.

Catharine was seasick as well, but after a few days she stopped throwing up and left her cabin to sit and sew or stroll the deck with her arm in Thomas's. She discovered how pessimistic he could be. There was nothing for him to do except watch the waves and worry about Catharine and the unknown life ahead.

Catharine talked about the good things that might happen, although she admitted in a letter to her mother that such "glorious tales" as she told "in all probability will never be realized."

She amused herself with the captain's bird, a goldfinch, who sang when she gave him biscuit to eat. As with Downy the field mouse, she observed him closely. She noted in her journal the day he started singing all day long. He sensed they were near land at last.

IMMIGRANT SHIPS

Catharine's travelling conditions were far better than most new colonists. She had a proper cabin and decent food. On other ships, poorer emigrants travelled "steerage" in the hold, sleeping on plank bunks crammed into the space, with no fresh air, awash in dirty water, sharing the bad food with the rats. Many died before they ever reached the new land.

Catharine was one of about 52,000 people who officially landed in Quebec in 1832, a peak year for the flood of immigrants that came in that decade.

Quarantine

FIRST IMPRESSIONS

Catharine looked at the scenery as they continued upriver. She was happier when the south shore showed signs of people, the sun glittering off the tin roofs of churches. She noted the buildings painted in bright colours but preferred the natural tones of plain wood shingles.

She thought gardens could be made prettier if more were done with what she called good taste. She had yet to learn that survival took most of a settler's effort.

Grosse-île

The ship sailed into the Gulf of the St. Lawrence river. Catharine found the mountains of the rocky north shore awe-inspiring.

At swampy Pointe au Bic, Thomas was allowed to land, but the captain ordered Catharine to stay aboard, and she did. To console her, Thomas brought back a bouquet of flowers; sweet pea, orchis, pulmonaria, and some blossoms she had never seen before.

Waiting to pass medical inspection at Grosse-Île, they all had to stay aboard. From up on deck the island looked green and picturesque, but Catharine learned the buildings were crowded with people suffering in filth and hunger, dying of cholera, smallpox, typhus and measles. Cholera raged in Quebec City too, so they did not go ashore there either.

As they sailed on, Catharine watched white beluga whales swim alongside. A tiny bird flying over reminded her of a goldcrested wren. She was never bored with nature. She wrote in her letters home: "The simplest weed that grows in my path, or the fly that flutters about me, are subjects for reflection, admiration and delight."

SAVING HER LIFE

Catharine lay in bed at the Nelson Hotel fighting for her life. The awful diarrhea and vomiting of cholera left her muscles racked with cramps and her whole body dehydrated.

Thomas was panicky at the thought of losing Catharine. He brought a doctor, who applied what remedies he could, but he had seen many hundreds die.

Catharine survived because Jane Taylor, sister of the hotel's owner, and two Irish girls who worked there, risked their own lives. They nursed her around the clock, giving her drinks, keeping her clean and saving her from injury when she thrashed in pain.

Custom House Square in 1830.

Custom House Square in Montreal, where Catharine landed

First Days On Land

They docked in Montreal on August 21st, 1832. While Thomas argued with customs officials about lost luggage, Catharine explored.

She was disappointed in the hot streets and stone houses. They had wide iron stairs and balconies but no flowers or trees for shade. Loud laughter came from crowded inns, but people looked sad. The doors of many houses were decorated in black. Cholera deaths had been devastating here too.

Later they met a man returning to England, giving up farming. It was too hard. He blamed Cattermole for lying. After listening to him rant, they decided he had foolishly thought it would be easy. As Thomas said "Persons are apt to deceive themselves...and... will only read and believe those things that accord with their wishes." The Traills would not make the same mistake.

"We are prepared to meet with many obstacles and endure considerable privations, though I dare say we may meet with many unforeseen ones," Catharine wrote. That prediction proved true the very next day. She woke up with a high fever. Cholera!

Heading Towards Sam's

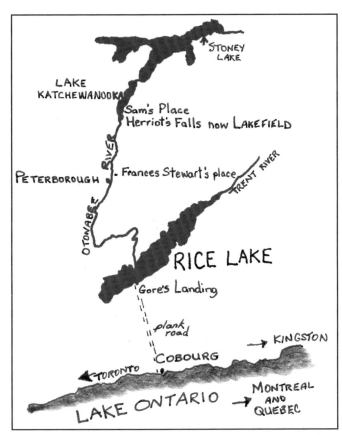

A map of Catharine's journey to her new home

Catharine didn't die. After seven days, the doctor told Thomas to take her away. Although so weak she could hardly stand, they drove in a bumpy stagecoach round the Lachine rapids to catch the steamboat. They would travel by stages, riding and sailing to Cobourg, in what is now Ontario, along the plank road, then up the Otonabee River to Peterborough.

Catharine was delighted to sail past neat, prosperous farms, claimed from the wilderness in the last thirty years. Rich harvests of apples and plums grew in the orchards. Hanks of wool yarn coloured with plant dyes hung on fences to dry.

In the dooryards of the wood frame houses, girls spun wool with big walking wheels. Catharine noted this was a good way to show off one's figure to the boys.

She also noticed graveyards. Five years later she wrote; "I perhaps overlooked at that time the labour, the difficulties, the privations... I saw it only at a distance of many years, under a high state of cultivation, perhaps in the hands of their children, or children's children, while the toilworn parent's head was low in the dust."

23

Although it was generally safe to drink water from the springs and streams, most adults drank beer, cider or wine. These drinks were often made at home. Stronger distilled drinks such as whisky and gin were commonly available in the many taverns and inns, and they were cheap. Though they had medicinal qualities as relaxants and sterilizers, these "hard" liquors were also addictive. Rowdy, irresponsible behaviour due to too much alcohol was a problem that spoiled the party at the end of many work gatherings or "bees". Lumber camps often forbade liquor because of the dangers.

Rougher Travel

Catharine was used to comfort because of her class. Now she squashed into a carriage with nine people, some with whooping cough. At night, she took whatever bed was offered, fleas and all. She quickly swallowed awful food, rushing to catch the next stage.

The steamboat going up the Otonabee river got stuck in the mud before reaching the regular stopping place. The boats meeting it had to be rowed further down river. They arrived at night, the rowers drunk and arguing. Then they abandoned the steamboat passengers.

Thomas persuaded one of their fellow travellers who knew the area to walk them through the forest to Peterborough, nearly five kilometres.

They slogged along the rough trail in the dark. Crossing a creek, Catharine slipped off a log bridge into the water. She struggled on, her sopping skirt tangling her ankles.

When they finally reached the inn, it was full. Exhausted, Catharine pleaded for a resting place, saying she was Sam Strickland's sister. Hearing her pathetic tale, the innkeepers took pity and gave up their bed to the Traills.

Joyful Reunion

GOVERNMENT ADVICE

On no account enter into any final engagement for your lands or farms without personal examination, and then be certain of the following qualifications:

1. A healthy situation [meaning not in a swamp or disease area]
2. Good land [meaning able to grow crops]
3. A pure spring, or running stream of water
4. In the neighbourhood of good, moral and religious state of society, and schools for the education of your children
5. As near good roads and water transport as possible, saw and grist mills
6. A good title [meaning check the seller really owns the land]

Word was sent to Sam. Two days later, Catharine jumped out of bed at midnight to hug the brother she had not seen for seven years. He had been so excited to learn that his sister was in Canada that from Herriot's Falls, he had madly paddled his canoe eighteen kilometres, in the dark, through the rapids. It had never been done before. William Reid, who was with him, hoped it never would be again.

Sam did not know Catharine had married, nor that she was emigrating. Letters had never reached him. He welcomed the Traills enthusiastically. He would find them a place to stay and show them how to choose land. Catharine was pleased to find herself in a whirlwind of organization and advice.

Sam's storekeeper friends Ephraim and Ann Sandford offered to shelter them. They also boarded with one of the first families to settle there, Thomas and Frances Stewart. This began a friendship between Mrs. Traill and Mrs. Stewart that continued the rest of their lives.

25

FRANCES BROWN STEWART
1794-1872

Born in Dublin, Ireland, Frances was raised by her cousin, author Harriet Beaufort. She married Thomas Alexander Stewart in 1816, and in 1822, with three baby daughters, they came to the Peterborough area as one of the earliest pioneer families. She survived the loneliness of the bush and understood the difficulties Catharine would face. Her many letters, describing life in Douro with other settler families like the Stricklands and the Langtons, were eventually published by her daughter Ellen Dunlop as *Our Forest Home* in 1899.

Kindred Spirit

Catharine stepped into Frances Stewart's warm log house and gazed with delight. So this is what a home in the backwoods could be like. Flowers, crystals, chunks of lichen, squirrel skins, eagle feathers and books surrounded her. Pottery and baskets and a cradle made by Anishinabe craftspeople were in use. In one spot, amazingly, stood a piano.

Frances loved all the same things as Catharine, including children. The Stewart little ones surged round, curious about their new neighbour, and Catharine began telling them stories. Thirteen-year-old Eleanor enjoyed them too and claimed Catharine as a friend of her own.

Mr. Traill and Mr. Stewart, both named Thomas, also found a lot in common, and the two families were involved in each other's lives ever after, visiting back and forth when possible and writing letters often in between.

An illustration from Catharine's book
The Backwoods of Canada

Homestead In Douro

Catharine had admired the flat plains near Rice Lake, but Sam thought they would often get sick down there, so Thomas bought land near Herriot's Falls to go with his free land from the government, which was Lot 19, Concession 7, Douro Township.

Their property went right down to Lake Katchewanooka. They could travel by canoe, and Sam and his wife Mary lived right next door, handy to ask the hundreds of questions about this new way of life.

But the best way to learn was on the spot, so the Traill's hired a driver and wagon to cart their belongings along the road to Sam's.

Catharine wrote: "Imagine you see me perched up on a seat composed of carpet-bags, trunks and sundry packages, in a great, rough box set on wheels, the sides being pegged in, so that more than once I found myself in an awkward predicament, owing to the said sides jumping out. In the midst of a deep mud hole, out went the front board and in went the driver!"

FREE LAND TO START

Because Thomas Traill was an army officer, he was entitled to a grant of land of one hundred acres and the right to buy more at fixed prices. To get final title to his land, he had to perform "settlement duties". This meant clearing trees and bush along the concession line in front of the lot at least "6 rods wide" (about 30 metres). These strips eventually became Ontario's country road system. He had to build a shanty 18 feet x 20 feet (about 5.5 metres x 6 metres) and clear at least two acres for planting (approximately 7800 square metres), all within two years.

Peace and No Regrets

After getting lost more than once, the wagon driver finally dumped them and their luggage at the edge of the lake and drove off in the dark. While Thomas searched for the lights of Sam's house so he could call over, Catharine sat on a moss-covered rock surrounded with her bags and boxes and thought of everything that had brought her to this moment.

Despite being hungry, tired and bruised, despite the knowledge that she would likely never again see her old home, despite the vast forest darkness, she suddenly felt connected to this new land.

"A holy and tranquil peace came down upon me, soothing and softening my spirits into a calmness that seemed as unruffled as was the bosom of the water that lay stretched out at my feet."

YOU CALL THIS A ROAD?

Usually cheerful Catharine also wrote home: "Much as I had seen and heard of the badness of the roads in Canada, I was not prepared...(for it was) little more than an opening hewed out through the woods, the trees being felled and drawn aside... beset with innumerable obstacles in the shape of loose blocks of granite and limestone; to say nothing of fallen trees, big roots, mudholes and corduroy bridges, over which you go jolt, jolt, jolt, till every bone in your body feels as if it were going to be dislocated...sometimes I laughed because I would not cry."

"BUSH PUDDING"

Catharine's shopping list of rice, sugar, currants, pepper and mustard might arrive all jumbled into one mess because the bags broke, jolting along the road. She wrote home making a joke of the new "recipe" to be added to one of the famous cookbooks of the time. In reality it was a serious hardship, for no one could afford to waste food.

Staying With Sam and Mary

The Traills crowded in with the Stricklands until a nearby log house was left empty. They began to learn Canadian-style farming. Thomas started underbrushing, chopping small branches and shrubs, ready to fell trees in the winter for their own log house.

Catharine worked alongside Mary, learning to make potato rising for bread, cook a shanty loaf in an iron bake-pot on the fire, dip and pour candles. She learned to make do when the shopping list she sent down to Peterborough came back without half the items, because there was no pork available or the mill was not grinding so there was no flour.

The Stricklands' three children were delighted to play with their Aunt Traill. They were all under four years old, and Mary was relieved to have another pair of eyes to make sure that the toddlers did not fall into the fire, eat poisonous berries or try to chop wood before they were strong enough not to chop toes instead.

Hortus Siccus

DRIED PLANTS

To preserve plants for cooking, crafts or study, the water must be removed. Plants for cooking, such as parsley, might be hung in a bunch by the fireplace, or in the sunshine.

Plants for crafts or study were placed between sheets of paper or cotton (Catharine recommended cotton) then put between the pages of a book. More books would be piled on top for weight, or it would be wedged back on the shelf. After a week or two, the flattened plant could be pasted into a scrapbook.

Catharine escaped the dim cabin for the outdoors as often as she could, taking her niece and nephew for walks. She began collecting seed pods, colourful leaves and fall flowers.

She wished she had paid more attention when her sister had given lessons in botany. Although she could see some that were like the English plants she knew, she felt very ignorant. She longed for a reference book to look up names, but such a thing was not to be had until she visited Frances again.

In her letters home, she wrote of ferns, twice-flowering yellow violets and purple Michaelmas daisies. She gave unfamiliar plants names of her own, calling herself a sort of "floral godmother" and hoping no one would mind.

She pressed her finds between the pages of a large ledger writing book Thomas had brought and made notes. Her "hortus siccus", her dried plant collection, became the basis for writing detailed flower studies.

An illustration of carnations by Susanna Moodie

My Dearest...

SAVING PAPER

Letters were paid for by the person receiving them, and the cost varied according to distance and how many pages. To save money, Catharine wrote neatly down the page one way, then turned the page sideways and wrote across her first lines. Sometimes she turned the page again and wrote on a diagonal.

By 1851, the sender paid for the postage, shown by a stamp stuck on the outside of the sheet, or eventually envelope. Catharine's friend, Sir Sandford Fleming, designed the the first Canadian postage stamp, the Three-Pence Beaver.

Catharine wrote more than five hundred letters in her lifetime. The only way to stay in touch then was by mail. Writing letters also helped to deal with things like homesickness. In tough times, Catharine described her surroundings and shaped events into positive or funny stories. Telling about new experiences, such as static electricity sparks when she brushed her hair and sleigh riding when the snow came, lifted her spirits. Attitude could make the difference in whether settlers survived and succeeded, and Catharine worked on her outlook in her letters to England.

Her letters to friends in Canada, and to her sister Susanna, who had arrived in Canada but decided to stay near Cobourg, were more natural and full of affection for the recipients. Despite the cost of paper, her thoughts flowed freely; from the wonders of nature to the price of carpet material, from someone's illness to reflections on religion. She would apologize for not writing sooner and go on for several sentences after she declared she had to stop. As she said, "Brevity...is not one of my excellences."

BIRTHING BABIES

Women and babies often died during a birth or soon afterward. There were no modern medical treatments such as blood transfusions, oxygen, incubators or antibiotics.

If the mother could not feed her baby her breastmilk, and no other woman could "wet nurse" the baby, it might be fed gruel—watery oatmeal broth—but it usually died anyway.

Catharine did not lose any babies at birth. She also paid for the services of Dr. John Hutchison, in Peterborough, for her first baby, and several others.

Being a Mother

Catharine loved children but did not write about expecting their first baby. It was considered too rude to directly mention sex, pregnancy and actual birth.

Sam's wife, Mary, was pregnant with her fourth child, so Catharine saw how things were done in the new country. Babies were "swaddled" in wrappings and slept in baskets or wooden cradles, unless tucked in with their parents to keep warm. They nursed, sucking milk from their mother's breasts.

Catharine gave birth to nine children, her first, James, when she was age thirty-one, her last Walter, when age forty-six. Every year and a half or so, there was a new baby. Whatever Catharine did, she often had a newborn in her arms or a toddler in her lap, trying to get comfy round her big belly.

She did have some household help. Isabella Gordon lived in as nursemaid when James was born. Thomas's cousin Jane came from Orkney on a long visit after Katie was born. Later, the older ones helped with the little ones.

Building a Log House

While Catharine worked with her sister-in-law, Thomas hired men and cleared and chopped trees to build their house.

Trouble struck. Their ox team wandered away, and no logs could be hauled. They lost time until Sam could lend his team. Neighbours came to a bee to raise the walls, but the man hired to saw the floor boards didn't come.

Winter cold suddenly froze the mixture of lime and clay used for chinking between logs and plastering the walls. The women tried baking and boiling it, but a new lot had to be made. Then the man smoothing the plaster gashed himself with the blade.

They kept working. Thomas walked all the way from Peterborough carrying window glass himself so it wouldn't break.

Finally, December 1833, the house was ready. They named it "Westove", after Thomas's old home. Moving day was as cold as the one to Reydon Hall and "Various were the valuable articles of crockery-ware that perished in their short journey through the woods."

But at last Catharine sat down and wrote a letter describing her very own house.

FOOD FOR THOUGHT

Catharine wrote to her English sisters that she cooked "some huge joints of salt pork, a peck of potatoes, rice pudding and a loaf that was as big as an enormous Cheshire cheese" (about the size of a small car wheel) to feed the sixteen men and families that came to help.

After the bee, Catharine felt disappointed. She still had illusions from Cattermole's book about how fast a log house could be built. This experience showed her the need for more realistic guides for pioneers.

Westove, Douro
"Our Nutshell"

FANCIER START

A Franklin stove was more efficient than an open fireplace to heat the house. It used less wood, and the warmth rising upstairs through the stove pipe made the bedrooms more comfortable in winter, when the temperature could drop so low that the water in a washing jug froze, or frost from the condensing breath of the sleepers appeared on the blankets.

Catharine wrote "our nutshell" to describe her tiny house, but knowing her mother would compare it unfavourably to Reydon Hall, she tried to make the most of Westove's features.

The house was about 4.25 metres by 6 metres. The ground floor had a bedroom, a kitchen with a pantry and a sitting room, called a parlour, which also boasted a closet. A Franklin stove in the parlour provided heat that also warmed the upstairs through the stovepipe. At the windows hung handsewn curtains of green cambric and white muslin. A glass pane in the door gave a view of the lake.

Catharine admitted the walls were rough, but they were mostly covered up by Thomas's maps and prints and his shelves of books in several languages.

While the snowflakes flew outside, Catharine sat on a white painted chair at her pine table, writing cheerfully about Thomas reading an Italian novel, baby James rocking in his cradle and future plans with new friends.

A Franklin stove

A painting of Anishinabe women and children from 1826

Friends Among the First Peoples

Catharine's neighbours included several Anishinabe Indian families, particularly Mr. and Mrs. Peter Nogan, as they were known in English. The Traills and the Nogans visited, traded food, or borrowed household items from each other.

Catharine was interested in everything they had to show her about their way of life. Many things made sense to copy, such as wearing moccasins in the snow, carrying babies in cradleboards and using soft mosses as diapers. She learned more plants to use for medicines and preservatives. She bought things they made, a birchbark breadbasket and a knifetray decorated with quill beads and a toy canoe to send back to England.

The Anishinabe families had the same religion as the Traills, Christianity. Catharine loved their singing at the Sunday services. She liked the way they raised their children. She enjoyed their humour and the word pictures in their language. Looking at her bright blue eyes and rosy skin, they named her Peta-wan-noo-ka, which refers to the golden pink clouds at dawn.

CHANGING LIFESTYLES

The Anishinabe people's lands lay between northeastern Georgian Bay and eastern Lake Superior. After 1763, they sold some to the British Crown which allowed the Canada Company and others to divide and sell to the pioneers. Some Anishinabe kept their traditional hunting, fishing and fur trading life, but those in what became Southern Ontario gradually took up farming. Catharine uses the old spelling, "Chippewa", in her writing. They were also called Ojibwa.

Bush To Farmland

TREE LOVER

Catharine hoped to save some beech saplings in the middle of the yard from the fire, but though they were left unchopped, the heat of the fires killed them anyway. Larger trees would have been unsafe to save because they were too shallowly rooted and might blow down in a storm.

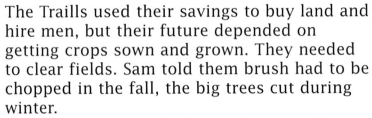

The Traills used their savings to buy land and hire men, but their future depended on getting crops sown and grown. They needed to clear fields. Sam told them brush had to be chopped in the fall, the big trees cut during winter.

In spring they held a logging bee. Neighbours came with ox teams to haul the trees not needed for fences or buildings into big piles. Then they burned them.

Catharine worried that if the breeze came up, the fire might shift to the forest, or the house. It was thrilling to see the big flames, but when all was charred and blackened, only dead tree stumps left, it looked so ugly Catharine couldn't help feeling sorry.

As soon as the ashes were cool and spread, Thomas and his helpers planted little hills of corn and pumpkins, potatoes and turnips, and scratched into the ground with a harrow to sow oats. These crops would not be overrun by wild plants, such as a "vile stinking thistle called fireweed" that would sprout now the sun could shine on it.

In the Garden

The red fox—a pesky predator

POULTRY AND PESTS

Catharine also took care of chickens, ducks, geese, and turkeys, birds raised for eggs, meat and feathers. During the day, a watch had to be kept for hawks that might swoop down and carry one off. At night they were shut up, but a fox or skunk might still dig a way in to the coop and kill them or take eggs.

Beside oats, corn, rye and barley, the settlers needed vegetables. Swatting away blackflies and mosquitoes, Catharine planted marrowfat peas, French, kidney and bush beans, scarlet and white runner beans, lettuce, melons and cabbages, all from seed.

She took strawberries, gooseberries, red currants, apple trees and grapes from the wild and transplanted them into her garden. Hop vines grew up the posts of the verandah built onto the front of the log cabin. Hops were "an excellent and indispensable article in every settler's house". They fermented into a "rising barm" used in bread and beer.

Catharine wove a twig fence around the garden and added bramble bushes. The raspberry and blackberry fruit provided dessert and jam, and their prickles kept the animals out. Part of the fence was moosewood, a shrub whose bark made cord for tying sacks or sewing birchbark baskets. For beauty and hummingbirds, she planted white and rose-blossomed honeysuckle.

But the transplant Catharine was happiest about was her sister Susanna, who moved to the land beside the Traills.

This historical plaque about Susanna is on land she once owned near Lakefield

THE AGUE

Malaria and similar diseases attack a person and give them high fever, delirium, sweating, shaking and weakness. They may even kill. The symptoms come back whenever a person is overstressed and weak.

Catharine had a theory that the root cellar where they stored potatoes, carrots and other vegetables, was full of "evil humours" from being flooded and so was the source of illness.

She may have been right, since malaria is spread by mosquitoes, which breed in standing water. The damp and rotting vegetable matter was certainly good for growing molds, which can also cause illness.

Happiness and Helping Hands

With Susanna nearby, Catharine got to know her little nieces, Catherine and Agnes. Susanna knew how her sister felt when she was homesick and was a help when trouble came.

One of the worst things that could happen to pioneer families was suddenly all falling ill, too sick to nurse each other or go for help. In their second year as settlers, a fever called ague, which we know as malaria, hit them all.

Sam's wife Mary and Susanna nursed the Traills, dosing them with calomel, castor oil and quinine, a medicine made from tree bark. Catharine was out of bed in a couple of weeks, but Thomas suffered fevers and great weakness the rest of the year and baby James was poorly too.

While the Traills were still ill, they struggled to help the Moodies when they caught the ague. John was still not on his feet when Susanna gave birth again. Little wonder that Catharine did not write anything, not even a letter, about her new nephew for several months!

Days Of Work and Wonder

SWIMMING SQUIRREL

One summer evening, Catharine, Thomas and James were paddling home in the canoe when they caught up to a red squirrel swimming. This was most unusual. They watched it while they rested their paddles. The squirrel then scrambled onto a paddle, jumped on James' head, onto Catharine's shoulder and back in the water again, as if to show it would allow nothing to get in the way of its journey to the shore!

Catharine's hands were never still, churning butter, knitting socks, quilting petticoats for warmth under winter dresses, wiping porridge from her son's face, massaging her husband's sore shoulders.

But even on her busiest days, she stayed her steps to watch the wildlife. Chickadees frolicked in the cedars. Baby woodpeckers poked their heads out from their nest in an old pine. She was so enchanted with the red squirrels that she let them steal the sunflower seeds she was drying to feed the hens.

She studied animal bodies when hunters brought them and sent skins and feathers to her sisters. Her letters had detailed descriptions of her favourite new flowers, waterlilies and columbines.

Thomas listened to her discoveries, but could not find pleasure in them. He saw it was a mistake coming to the backwoods at his age. Despite his utmost efforts, the farm was not succeeding. He had borrowed money. Now it had to be paid back. In 1835, he advertised the farm for sale, but nobody bought it.

Catharine needed to earn money again. Naturally, she turned to her pen.

A Book Of Letters

COPYRIGHT

The person who holds the copyright to a work is the person who should receive money any time a new edition is produced. In Catharine's time, copyright laws were not as strict as they are now and, because of distance and the difficulty of communication, it was impossible to find out if others had "pirated" a work until it was too late. Editions of several of Catharine's works appeared without her permission.

Authors now have a similar problem because the Internet makes it easy to copy work without paying the original author.

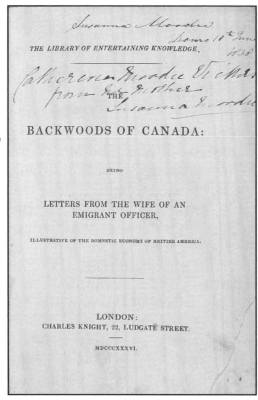

The title page of *The Backwoods of Canada*.
This was Susanna's personal copy,
which she later gave to her daughter.

Catharine checked with her sister Agnes in England to see if a new book for emigrants might sell. It would be a record of her own experience and full of practical tips to help others prepare for the difficulties of pioneering. Agnes thought it was a good idea, "as Canada mania is still strong".

Most of Catharine's story was already written in her letters home. She sent more notes from her journal. Agnes and Jane puzzled out her handwriting, made a good copy and sent the manuscript to a publisher named Charles Knight. He liked it and the book came out in 1836, titled: *The Backwoods of Canada: Being Letters from the Wife of an Emigrant Officer, Illustrative of the Domestic Economy of British America*.

Newspaper reviews praised the book "for its spirit and truth". With German and French translations, it became a bestseller on both sides of the Atlantic ocean.

The Otonabee River in spring flood

Growing Family, More Troubles

Being a bestseller did not make Catharine rich. Instead of having a royalty agreement, which would give her money for each copy sold, she exchanged the copyright of her book for a flat amount. It was soon gone.

The Traills' farm problems worsened. The weather was either so bad the crops failed or so good they had a bumper harvest so prices dropped. Getting crops to market was slow, because canals on the Otonabee River were not yet built. People stopped coming to Douro because of the bad times and diseases, like cholera, so Thomas still could not sell the farm.

Catharine's second child, Kate, was born in March 1836, and a year later came Harry. Hoping to get a government office job for Thomas, or some money, Susanna sent a letter to the Lieutenant Governor, explaining that Catharine, though famous, was almost starving. Nothing happened.

Catharine scoured the woods for plants to eat and invented new recipes for pork and potatoes, their basic food. Then, in the winter of 1837, she had a worry of a different kind.

THE TRENT CANAL

Water travel was best for lumber, goods and people, but rapids and waterfalls blocked the way. Canals were channels dug around these problems. By making gates that could hold the water in certain parts of the channel, boats could be lifted up or down to the level of the next lake.

The Otonabee is part of the Trent-Severn system, which links Lake Ontario (at Trenton) to Lake Huron (at Port Severn, Georgian Bay). Started in 1830, but not finished till 1920, it is 388 kilometres long, rises 181 metres at the top (Balsam Lake) and drops 79 metres down to Lake Huron.

41

MACKENZIE'S FIGHT

Some of Upper Canada's top officials were only over from England for a short stay and did not understand the needs of the people. There was a system of picking favourites for government paid jobs, or for giving land, that made many people angry. William Lyon Mackenzie, an excitable newspaper writer, was first mayor of Toronto and an elected member of the Provincial Assembly. He wanted to reform the style of government. When he felt his ideas were ignored, he led eight hundred men, armed mostly with farm tools, to try and take over the government buildings.

It Might Be War

Catharine sat up late the night of December 7, 1837, writing in her journal. Thomas was leaving at daybreak to fight against rebels who were attacking the government buildings in Toronto. Rumour said the city was burnt, people killed, that Americans might invade. Thomas was an army officer. It was his duty to defend Queen Victoria's Canadian government. Praying for the safety of his wife and three small children, he disappeared down the road in the season's first snow.

Catharine agreed he must do his duty, but she was still frightened. How would she manage? There were paths to be shovelled to the barn, animals and children to be fed, fires to keep going. What if the rebels came to Douro? What if Thomas didn't come back?

Other wives were going through the same thing. John Moodie was hopping around on crutches because of a broken leg, but he went anyway. Catharine invited Susanna and her children to visit with her. Together they worried and worked out survival plans.

A painting of fighting at Dickinson Landing during the rebellion

What a Relief!

A few days later, Catharine looked anxiously down the snowy hill. Mary Strickland's sister was trudging up. Good news or bad? Good. The men would return soon, the rebellion had failed. Catharine drove Susanna and her four children through the starry

night back to their own house. Under the buffalo robes in the sleigh, they giggled with happiness.

It was a special Christmas feast that year, and Susanna's family joined the Traills. Catharine decorated the cabin with hemlock branches and dried cranberries. The children enjoyed maple sugar treats. They all played in the snow, both the men on crutches now since Thomas had fallen from a horse while away. They sang carols and offered prayers for everyone's health and safety.

That night, in her journal, Catharine wrote of the mixed feelings Christmas brought. She missed her other sisters, her mother and her dead father. She remembered the big parties when she was a little girl. All that was left of those fine times was her coral bead necklace, now glowing from the wreath of greenery in their tiny parlour.

Struggling On

BELOVED WIFE

Thomas lost faith in his dream of providing a good life and knew he was difficult to live with because of it. He wrote in his journal, thanking God for providing him with his beloved wife, a woman of "admirable temper and highest moral worth".

Catharine looked at Thomas sitting with slumped shoulders. It worried her to see him so depressed, and his "wretched spirits" made him unable to do much. He was forty-five and desperate to quit farming. He wrote again to his grown sons in Scotland, but neither came to help.

Thomas envied his brother-in-law, John Moodie. He now worked as paymaster for the army in Belleville, a hundred miles away. No office job was found for Thomas.

Sometimes Catharine sent him to give Susanna a hand, because she worried about her as well. Susanna was running her farm herself, taking care of five children and also writing. Catharine worried too about her own baby, Anne, born in December 1838, and often ill. They still needed more money.

She sent a new book, a sequel to *The Backwoods*, to her sister in England, but this time Agnes didn't find a publisher. Eventually, *Chambers' Edinburgh Journal* published "Canadian Lumberers" and "The Mill of the Rapids: A Canadian Sketch", stories from the book, but it seems Catharine received no payment.

Moving On

SLIPPING STANDARDS

Catharine and Thomas were seriously concerned at how little time they could spend educating their children. Very few of all the skills in writing and languages that they had were getting passed on. Catharine even proposed starting a boarding school if Barbara Fotheringhame would come from Scotland to help. At one point, two of her children, Mary, twelve, and Willie, eleven, had to walk long distances for lessons, starting out at seven in the morning and not returning until seven at night.

Catharine told Thomas to take the only offer they got to buy their farm. If they moved to a village, he might find easier work. The children could go to school and learn more than just farm life.

They packed up in February, 1839. The Franklin stove and a sack of potatoes went to Susanna. Some goods were sold to the new homeowner. The clock ticked hollowly in the empty cabin as Catharine took a last, sad look at Westove. Then they sleighed down to a house the Stewarts lent them to live in for a while.

Being closer to Frances and her husband was comforting. Together they sewed and played with the babies, talked about books and plants and music. Catharine discussed her ideas for a story about lost children, always a worry to pioneer families. The Traills helped search for a child lost in the woods at least once. Catharine knew the kind of adventures they might have, and as soon as they were settled again she wanted to write them.

Life In Ashburnham Village

Catharine sent one short story about lost children back to Scotland. Then she wrote on different themes for a new magazine called *The Literary Garland*, published in Montreal by John Lovell. He welcomed stories by Canadian authors.

In October 1839, the Traills moved to Ashburnham, across the Otonabee River from Peterborough. The house had an orchard, which Thomas cared for, while Catharine planted a garden full of vegetables with bug-repelling marigolds and scented sweet peas.

Life was easier, except for their debts. The Traills were living on borrowed money. Thomas's pension was not enough to keep them. Until he could get a steady job, they did whatever they could to earn cash.

Catharine opened a day school, charging a fee for each pupil. She offered her skills as a midwife and nurse, helping women in childbirth. She sold homemade herbal medicines and the down feathers from her geese. Even little Katie helped, carrying chicken eggs to market.

While in Ashburnham, Catharine gave birth to her fifth child, Mary Helen Bridges Traill, October 30, 1840.

Catharine
Still Learning

FORMAL BOTANY

Different plants often have the same name. Catharine described a "vile, stinking thistle called fireweed". The provincial flower of the Yukon, the rose baywillow herb, is also called fireweed and is not a thistle or stinky.

To solve this problem, in 1793 Karl Linnaeus began a naming system, giving plants a "family" and "individual" name in Latin, an old unchanging language that many educated people knew. Plants are sorted according to details of structure. Catharine's fireweed was Erechtites hieracifolia, while the Yukon fireweed is fireweed is Epilobium augustifolium, the evening primrose family.

Linnaeus

Another book Catharine wanted to write was about plants. She wanted it to be scientifically correct but also enjoyable, with stories, poems and information like household uses. She loved an old English book like this called *The Natural History and Antiquities of Selborne*, by Gilbert White.

She knew plenty from her own observations, from other settlers and her Anishinabe friends, but to get the scientific part right, she began studying. She borrowed a book called *Flora Americae: Septentrionalis*, by Frederick Pursh. It was in Latin, but Thomas helped her understand it.

She wrote about each plant in her dried plant collection, using the proper terms. She exchanged letters with leading botanists in Scotland, such as John Macoun. He later came to Canada and became the government's top botanist.

How did she fit this in with all her other chores? Sometimes the older daughters of neighbours provided the extra hands needed for the care of the family. Though Catharine could pay them very little, she taught them a lot. Years later, many of them remembered her with love.

47

Sorrow In the Family

Like many poor families, the Traills were not healthy. They ate mostly potatoes and bread. They went all winter without fresh greens or fruit. Often too thinly dressed, they caught whatever ailments were going around. Infections that we can cure with antibiotic drugs killed people then.

Early in 1841, Catharine's baby, Mary Helen, died. Catharine cried but could not stop to grieve for long. Her four other children, all under eight, needed their mother. Thomas needed her too.

Before long, she was pregnant again. On November 7th, 1841, Mary Elizabeth Jane was born.

Catharine gave up teaching when she found she was expecting again. It was too tiring.

This new baby, Ellen, came a month early. She was named after Eleanor Stewart, who knit special tiny clothes for her, but the fragile baby died at three months. Catharine held Mary Elizabeth close and prayed often for all her children.

She never forgot her dead babies. Writing in her journal about helping a neighbour give birth, she remembered that very day would have been Mary Helen's third birthday.

CATHARINE'S NOTEBOOK

"Oatmeal gives strength and muscle more than wheaten flour. Oatmeal porridge once a day should enter into the daily food of young children."

A PLACE TO WORSHIP

Catharine wrote: "How deep is the silence of the forest! A strange sweet sense of restful stillness seems to come down upon the soul. One scarcely cares to tread too roughly, for it is as if the shadow of the mighty God of all creation were around us, calling for an unspoken prayer of praise and adoration. We stand beneath the pines and enter the grand pillared aisles with a feeling of mute reverence; these stately trunks bearing their plumed heads so high above us seem a meet roofing for His temple who reared them to His praise."

Catharine's Religious Faith

Catharine was a Christian. She believed in one powerful spirit, God, that created everything, including a special son, Jesus. Christians have faith that whatever happens in life is for a reason, even if it is hard to understand.

They believe if they are faithful and follow God's moral laws, there is a life after dying which is better and happier. Believing this helped Catharine all her life, especially when people she loved died.

Her beliefs coloured her way of looking at nature. To her, the wilderness showed God's lessons about how to live life. Plants like the Carpet Weed grew and flowered, no matter how hard the rocky ground. Birds cooperated in their migration flights.

In her writings, she would ponder why things were the way they were and marvel at living things as examples of God's great handiwork.

Christian organizations build churches for people to worship in. Whenever she could, Catharine went to a church. She missed this company when at Westove, Douro, but she found the deep woods gave her a similar feeling of comfort.

Back To Farming

STRONG CHARACTERS

Catharine was always conscious of how hard her children worked and grateful for their help. She had great faith in what children could learn and accomplish. In her novel, Canadian Crusoes, her teenage character Hector says: "After all, children can do a great many things if they only resolutely set to work and use the wits and the strength that God has given them to work with."

Early in 1844, the Traills had to move to an even cheaper place. The only choice was a farm again. At "Saville", Catharine got the garden started as soon as she could. Not only would they need the food but she would be less able to work as the spring came on because another baby was due. She also found it harder because of painful arthritis in her joints. She relied on James, 10, Katie, 7, and Harry, 6, to help her lift and carry. Annie, 4, had her share to do, distracting Mary, 2, from the pain of ear infections.

Right after moving in they all caught scarlet fever. Luckily, no one died.

Then came sad news from Belleville where all the Moodies now lived. Catharine's five-year-old nephew had drowned in the river. Catharine could not go to comfort her sister. She could only send her love and sympathy in letters.

The best thing that year was the safe arrival of the Traills' eighth child, William Edward, on July 26th.

GIFTS FROM REYDON

Many things were hard to get in the backwoods, which made them expensive. Sarah and Agnes sent shoes, stockings and bolts of fabric, such as cotton, calico, flannel, and muslin, to make shirts or dresses. Pins and needles, and other sewing supplies were included. Fashionable Agnes would send Catharine used clothes. She was grateful for ready made things, since she had so much sewing to do. Most appreciated were books. The twelve volumes of the *Lives of the Queens of England* written by Agnes and Jane were sent as they came out.

Forced From Saville

Catharine rarely went to bed before one o'clock. Burning pinewood knots for a smoky but cheap light, she sat writing for John Lovell's magazine. She made up cheerful stories, despite sore eyes, a rumbling tummy and aching hands. Lovell's prompt payment per page was essential to survive.

Even so, the children's clothes were ragged. Sometimes they could not go out into the cold to get wood and water, or to go to school because they had no shoes.

Catharine never wrote directly of her troubles to her sisters in England, but they partly guessed. They sent money when they could, and twice a year they sent a box of goods. Catharine admitted only to Susanna "The game of life seems to me a difficult one to play..."

It became more difficult in one blow when a man, who was building a mill they all needed, accidentally drowned. To help him, Thomas had promised to guarantee his loan from the bank. Now he had to pay up. The Traills used their crop money. Now they could not afford Saville, either.

Roblin's Mill in Ameliasburg, Ontario, now part of Black Creek Pioneer Village

51

Wolf Tower Summer

How would they manage now? Where could they live?

Catharine's friend and fan, George Bridges, had come from Jamaica, after reading *The Backwoods of Canada*. He had built a six-storey, octagonal house that Catharine named "Wolf Tower", but moved away again. He offered them this house on the Rice Lake Plains, rent-free. Catharine gratefully accepted the refuge.

"Just in time," Catharine wrote to Susanna, "for both my health and my spirits were sinking under the load of mental anxiety, more on his (Thomas's) account than the circumstances."

She spent a lot of time outdoors exploring this new countryside with the children, collecting more plants. She was too busy to write much, mostly letters and a song she called "Hurrah for the Forest", sung to an old Welsh tune. A version was printed in the *Peterborough Gazette* in 1846.

Thomas was grieving the death of Walter, his eldest son in Scotland, and they still had to work hard, but there was an air of summer camp at Wolf Tower. They were all healthier by the time they had to move again.

Next Stop:
"Mount Ararat"

The right to have a crest as part of a coat of arms was granted to Sir Alexander Traill in 1418. It was his reward for saving a member of the royal family by clinging to a rock after being shipwrecked. The crest is the tower on top and the Latin motto means "safety during danger". The family's silver spoons probably had the design as part of the handle.

The Traill family
coat of arms

In spring 1847, they rented another farm, "Mount Ararat", near Gore's Landing, Rice Lake. Once settled, Catharine got back to writing stories full of Canadian scenery and history, such as *The Interrupted Bridal: A True Story of the First Rebellion In the Colony*. It appeared in an English magazine two years later.

Catharine grieved for Thomas as more sad news came from Scotland. His second son had died.

Shortly afterward, heartbreaking news came from Peterborough. The disease typhus had killed Dr. John Hutchison, who had helped Catharine with five of her babies, and their dear friend Thomas Stewart, Frances's husband.

Once again, Catharine could not go to comfort people she loved. Thomas Traill, shabby, stooped and worn out, sadly attended Stewart's funeral alone, keeping his distance so as not to bring home disease.

But in their lively family there were still events that made Catharine laugh. Little Willie, three, took the last of the Traill crest silver spoons and planted them in the garden to make them grow. Unfortunately, he just couldn't remember where!

GROWING SOCIETY

The area around Rice Lake was developing steadily. When Catharine went to Peterborough in August 1848, to be under the care of a doctor for the birth of her ninth baby, she travelled in comfort on a regularly scheduled steamer.

Oaklands was near enough to the village of Gore's Landing for Catharine to attend newly-built St. George's Anglican church regularly. The Traills became friendly with more families, such as the Muchalls, into whose family Catharine's children James and Mary would eventually marry.

Move to Oaklands

Catharine's last baby, Walter, was born August 9, 1848. When he was nine months old, Mt. Ararat was unexpectedly sold.

Catharine was tired of moving. She found a log cabin with some land for sale nearby. They borrowed more money and Catharine convinced Thomas to cash out his commission in the army, which meant some money but no more pension, and they bought it.

Catharine, Thomas and the children, still tired and breathless from whooping cough, set to work once again, ploughing and planting. "Oaklands" had cleared fields and a garden, but it was on a hill. The wind whipped around it in the winter, making it hard to heat, and it was far from any woods for chopping logs for the fire.

However, at least it was theirs, as Catharine pointed out to Thomas, who was slipping deeper into depression and melancholy.

She tried as always to cheer him, singing in the evenings and telling stories that they all enjoyed. One in particular was growing into a complete book, the story of lost children that she called *Canadian Crusoes*.

St. George's Chruch, Gore's Landing. The church was rebuilt after the original wooden building the Traills would have attended burned down.

Sinking Deeper At Oaklands

Defoe's Robinson Crusoe

EXCITING NOVEL

Catharine's story was about three young teens who were lost in the wilderness. They rescue another girl their age and the four of them survive many life threatening adventures. She included many real details of forest life. *Canadian Crusoes* borrowed part of its title from a famous book by Daniel Defoe, *Robinson Crusoe*, the story of a sailor shipwrecked on an island. It was first published in 1719 and has been popular ever since.

Catharine pushed herself to write down twenty pages of *Crusoes* a day, despite great pain in her arm. She finished all 354 pages on September 27th, 1850. Agnes promised to find an English publisher as soon as possible.

It was something to hope for. Otherwise it had been a horrible year. Her brother Sam's wife, Mary, had died giving birth to their fourteenth child. His daughter's husband and baby had both died, and shortly afterward so did Sam's new baby and another child.

Catharine also felt sorry for Ellen Stewart, now Mrs. Dunlop, some of whose children had died. Ellen invited Annie, eleven, and Kate, fourteen, for the winter, so that she could teach them to spin.

It was two less mouths to feed. The Traills were still in debt. Thomas seemed paralyzed with despair. James, seventeen, and Harry, fourteen, ran the farm and resented having to work so hard. They wanted regular schooling and time to study properly. They were surly and disrespectful to their parents at times, which hurt Catharine's feelings. She wished it could be different for them.

A portrait of Susanna
from around 1860

ANSWERS

If Catharine's possessions had been seized by the bailiffs, she would have had five days to get them back before they were sold at a price determined by two appraisers other than the sheriff or bailiff. The money would then go to the person she owed, with any extra supposed to come back to her. The crops in the ground and the food in the pantry could be taken, but not the clothes they were wearing, or the bedding they were using.

"A Vessel Without a Pilot"

Catharine didn't know where to turn in the spring of 1852. "A vessel without a pilot", she wrote, in a desperate letter to Susanna. It was full of questions for Susanna's husband, now a sheriff in Belleville, about what the bailiffs could take to pay for debts. The crops in the ground? The food in the pantry? How could the Traills check on what happened to the money after the Sheriff's men sold the stove, or Thomas's watch and books?

Catharine could hardly think for worry. She could not write any stories at all. Katie was seriously ill, and no English publisher wanted *Canadian Crusoes*.

Her Bible reading reminded her that all things, troubles included, shall pass, but it was so hard to hold on until that happened.

She sold enough household goods to keep the bailiffs out, and finally *Canadian Crusoe*s sold. There was money coming, and Katie recovered.

Catharine's confidence returned, and she sent stories to Canadian magazines such as *Snowdrop*, for children, and the *Maple Leaf*.

TEACHING STORIES

In *The Governor's Daughter; or Rambles in the Canadian Forest*, Mary asks her nurse questions that she answers with stories about squirrel families and other animals. Stories like these were a way of teaching children who did not get to school on a regular basis.

The book was published in the United States as *Stories of the Canadian Forest; or Little Mary and Her Nurse*, but in England it came out as *Lady Mary and Her Nurse; or A Peep into the Canadian Forest*.

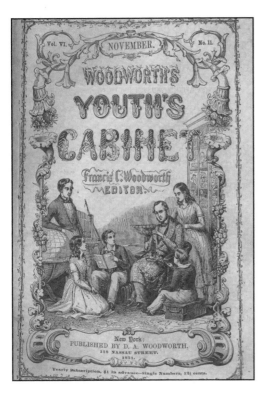

Slowly Getting Ahead

Catharine sold more. *Forest Gleanings*, thirteen stories about Rice Lake life, appeared in *Anglo-American Magazine*. The *Maple Leaf* published *The Governor's Daughter* in twelve installments.

Her sons finally went to school, James and Harry in Belleville, Willie and Walter locally. Daughters Kate, Anne and Mary managed the household. Catharine praised them because "they sort it all themselves", leaving her to work, resting her painful arthritic knees on the couch. When she could walk, she still went plant collecting.

By getting up a subscription list of people who promised to buy, she also persuaded a Toronto publisher to print *A Female Emigrant's Guide and Hints on Canadian Housekeeping*, her sequel to *The Backwoods*. Whether they dealt with loneliness or a house fire, Catharine advised women "...it is folly to fold one's hands and sit down to bewail in abject terror: it is better to be up and doing."

She never wanted anyone to just give up. *She* hadn't and now, halfway through her life, things were improving. But could she keep up her courage and her faith for the future?

Magazines like this one often had stories that continued in each issue. These stories were called serials.

Oaklands Demolished

CONSTANT DANGER

Both Catharine and Susanna suffered the loss of houses by fire. Everything being made of wood, it was a fairly common disaster. From the open fireplace, sparks could ignite rugs or clothing or smolder between floor boards. More frequent were chimney fires. Burning poorly dried wood, or woods with lots of resins like pine, left tarry residue which would catch fire and spread to the roof.

In August, 1857, Catharine wrote to Ellen Dunlop, "The whole of the crops this year are good—I never saw anything finer..." With the letter went Mary, 16, who was to stay. Catharine asked Ellen to take her daughter shopping for shoes and a dress.

Life was better for the Traills. Kate, 21, was housekeeping and sending displays of ferns to exhibitions. Willie, 13, was now away at school in Belleville. He stayed with James, 24, who was married and working in a store.

Catharine eagerly awaited a letter answering botanical questions from Dr. William Hincks, professor at University College, Toronto. Thomas was recopying Catharine's plant notes for a possible publisher.

Two weeks later, Catharine woke up smelling smoke. The house was burning. Thomas rushed upstairs to rescue Walter. Catharine roused Harry, Annie and Kate. The girls grabbed bedding, a few books and Catharine's notes, Harry hurled chairs outside, but there was no time to do more. The log cabin blazed up as they stood in the dark, silhouetted by the flames. Soon there was nothing but hot ash.

Scattered Refugees

PRIVACY STAMP

Sealing wax was used to hold a folded letter shut or close an envelope. The sender held a stick of beeswax to a flame until it dripped soft wax onto the paper, over the edges. Just before it cooled solid, a design could be pressed into it. The receiver knew the letter was unread by others if the seal was unbroken.

Queen Victoria's seal. Victoria was queen of England from 1837 to 1901.

The fire was catastrophic. They lost all the food stored for winter, clothes, quilts, carpets, candlesticks, kitchen utensils, furniture, and worst of all, the books and personal letters. But Catharine and Thomas thanked God that no one was killed.

There was no place available big enough for them all to stay together. Walter went to join Willie in Belleville with James, the girls went to friends. Catharine, Thomas and Harry stayed with Clinton Atwood, Anne's fiancé, and then with Sam and his new wife.

Friends gave them spare items. Catharine got busy sewing clothes and readying rags to be woven into a carpet. "We shall want it sadly wherever we are."

She wrote letters full of gratitude and would have written as well to the generous, but anonymous, friend who sent envelopes, sealing wax and two reams of paper. This person thoroughly understood what Catharine needed to keep going.

When Catharine's sister Agnes sent money, they decided not to rebuild Oaklands. Instead they bought land in the village now known as Lakefield, near Sam, and began saving up for a house.

Susanna (sitting) and John
(far right), around the year 1866

Grandchild and Spiritualism

That winter, four months after the fire, Catharine went to Belleville to visit her youngest boys. She stayed at Susanna's, which meant she had good care when she came down with bronchitis. She hadn't quite recovered when James' wife went into early labour with Catharine's first grandchild. Catharine got out of bed and went to help.

Susanna and John were involved in spiritualism, supposedly communicating with dead people. Susanna got Catharine to try it and felt that Catharine had talent as a medium, connecting them with their dead children. Susanna thought it helped Catharine get over a fear of death, but it is hard to know how seriously Catharine took spiritualism. She did not practice it after she returned to Thomas.

Because Thomas was depressed and in poor health, Catharine was relieved when Sam offered to have her daughter Anne and Clinton's wedding at his house in May, 1858.

Later that year, she borrowed Park Cottage in Peterborough from Frances Stewart. Finally, she and Thomas, Kate and Mary could live together again.

LOVING MEMORIAL

Today we might call Thomas's state of mind chronic depressive illness and he might be treated with drugs to help. Catharine saw to the heart of the person suffering.

She wrote: "Let me as a wife, and now a widow bear testimony to my husband's worth. With some foreign eccentricities of manner & some faults of nervous irritability of constitution, he was a true-hearted, loyal gentleman, faithful in deed and word—a kind & benevolent disposition, a loving father, husband and friend—a scholar and a true gentleman, whose virtues will be remembered long after his faults have been forgotten."

.

Catharine was left alone by Thomas's death, but she had much still to achieve in her life.

Last Chapter As a Wife

Catharine knew that her husband and her second son irritated each other, but Harry, now twenty-two, made both parents proud, camping at Oaklands and working the land. Thomas, sixty-five, wrote: "Harry's energy in the management of the farm is beyond all praise... I am happy to believe his heart is better than his temper."

He worked with Harry, but became too ill when winter returned.

To ease Thomas's mind as he lay helpless in bed, Catharine wrote down the story of his early years. His father had left him the Scottish property with huge debts. Thomas's last hope was that it could eventually be sold, leaving a little money. While he was ill, he learned there would be nothing. He died June 21, 1859.

Grieving Catharine wrote: "God in his wisdom thought it meet to take from me the much beloved Partner of my life. Twenty-seven years we walked together as friends."

Even Susanna never understood the depth of Catharine's feeling for Thomas. Catharine wore black mourning clothes for many years after and never remarried.

New Westove

Working for the New Westove

After Thomas's burial, Catharine rented rooms in Lakefield. Mary, who was teaching school, could live with her, as well as Kate, who became chief housekeeper, and Willie, fifteen. Willie, though, was often away with Harry. Walter, twelve, lived with Anne and her husband.

Catharine, now fifty-seven, yearned for her own place, and her family together, but had too little money. Even if Oaklands were to be sold, Catharine, as a widow, would get only one third of its value, so she rented it out.

Once again, she was "up and doing" rather than bemoaning her fate. She took a job she hated, sewing men's trousers. She made more pressed flower folios to sell.

Catharine's botanical work interested Lady Charlotte Greville in England. She sent a screw press to Catharine, who was delighted. This solved the problem of weights, since she had lost so many books in the fire.

Lady Greville also got her a grant of £100. Catharine could build her house at last. Thinking of Thomas, she named it "Westove".

They all moved into Westove in the spring of 1860 and planted the garden with everything from potatoes to polypodies—woodland ferns.

ADVENTURERS

Willie was hired as an apprentice clerk for the Hudson's Bay Company. Taken on at first because of recommendations that Catharine asked for from family connections in the Company, he eventually worked his way up to be Chief Trader at Lesser Slave Lake.

Walter also started as an apprentice clerk. He grew to be an independent businessman involved in wheat exports. Walter's biography was was published in 1970 as *In Rupert's Land; Memoirs of Walter Traill.*

No One Has It Easy

Catharine wished the roof of Westove could protect her children from being hurt, or that she had the means to ease their troubles when they were. They always had her sympathy and helping hands if she could get to them.

She nursed Anne's four-year-old boy, Henry devotedly but could not prevent his death from scarlet fever.

James was often ill, and four of his children died as infants.

Mary married and already had three children when it became clear her husband was an alcoholic. He was unable to hold a job and often behaved crazily.

Harry moved around a lot because his health was not strong enough for him to keep farming, particularly after a bad accident with a horse. After his marriage, he worked in Kingston as a prison guard.

Willie went west to the prairies with the Hudson's Bay Company. Walter followed him. They wrote letters back, telling tales of dangerous journeys and wild buffalo hunts. Catharine prayed for their safety and worked their adventures into a story called *Our Prairie Home.*

William Traill and his family in 1894

The Wildflower Book

LITHOGRAPHY

Lithography is a way of making pictures that can be printed. The artist draws on a piece of limestone with a greasy crayon or paints with an oily wash. Then the stone is washed in an acid solution that allows only the design to hold printer's ink. Paper laid on top and rolled will then carry the design. Many copies can be made. Eventually the stones can be reground then painted on again. Alois Senfelder, a German playwright, invented the technique in 1790. Later, zinc plates were used instead of limestone.

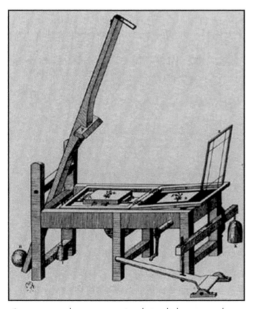

A manual press used in lithography

Catharine still longed to have her plant studies published. An early ecologist, she knew that many species, plant and animal, would disappear with their habitat. She wanted to "foster a love" for Canadian plants, before they were "swept away" by the "onward march of civilization". Publishers didn't care.

Catharine's niece, Agnes Moodie Fitzgibbon, who was an artist, suggested they do it themselves.

She talked people into subscribing for the first printing of a shorter book, an illustrated wildflower guide. John Lovell agreed to produce five hundred copies. Agnes painted the pictures for the new process of lithography, but she was unhappy with the reproduction. Rather than have a poor book, she learned to lithograph herself and printed five thousand pictures, one by one! Then she sat down, and helped by her daughters, coloured each picture by hand.

Catharine reviewed the notes she had spent thirty years collecting to choose the best descriptions of appearance and growth, the best scientific information and the most interesting stories about the chosen flowers.

Losing Sam and James

Agnes Moodie
Fitzgibbon

Catharine needed Agnes's energy during the wildflower book's preparation, because family matters took much of her own.

Soon after she learned that her mother, ninety-two, had died, Sam, sixty-two, her dynamic, kind and supportive younger brother, developed diabetes, which was then untreatable. He died in January of 1867.

Her son James's frequent illness became clearly tuberculosis, which was not curable. Catharine went to nurse him right after Sam's death.

Just as Catharine took comfort in religion, so did James. Catharine wrote to Frances, "I no longer grieve and mourn—we hold sweet counsel together—nor does he fear to think of the certainty of death."

James said goodbye to his wife and children, his sister Kate read him a hymn, and Catharine sat beside him as he breathed his last prayers in the early morning of April 14th, 1867.

And in the endless cycle of nature that Catharine understood so well, as she was losing her oldest child, she became grandmother to another. Mary had another baby girl, and Catharine wrote to Frances that she "was the prettiest I ever saw!"

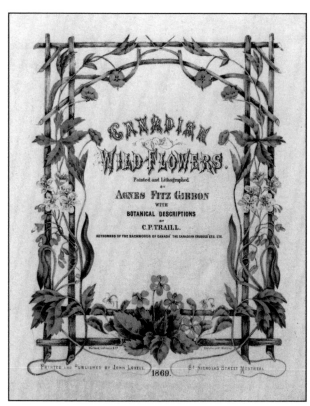

A Lovely Canadian Book

When *Canadian Wild Flowers* came out in 1868, a year after Confederation, it was a complete success and quickly went into more printings. The *Montreal Daily News* called it a "beautiful work" and "a most valuable addition to the literature of Canada".

Catharine, knowing the painstaking care she and Agnes had put in, was annoyed at the number of printing errors, though pleased by the sales.

It was now thirty-eight years since she had come to Canada. Catharine continued to write to leading scientists such as George Lawson, founder of the Botanical Society of Canada, which advised farmers and made plant catalogues. He was professor of natural history at Queen's College (now Queen's University) in Kingston.

She hoped his support and that of John Dawson, principal of McGill College (now McGill University) in Montreal, and Professor William Hincks, of the University of Toronto, would help get her longer work on plants published as well.

CONFEDERATION

Upper and Lower Canada (Ontario and Quebec), Nova Scotia and New Brunswick joined together July 1st, 1867 to become one country, the Dominion of Canada. Sir John A. Macdonald became the first Prime Minister.

People were especially proud to be able to buy Canadian made books on Canadian subjects.

PUNISHMENT FOR CRIME

Even children could be sent to jail, where conditions for all were extremely harsh. Prisoners had to work, often at stonebreaking or other hard labour, though girls and women did laundry and needlework. They were fed plain food in limited amounts. No talking or communicating in any way with other prisoners was allowed. Those who were caught were flogged.

Peter Charbonneau, aged ten, was serving a seven year sentence for stealing. He was publicly lashed for "staring, winking and laughing".

A hangman's noose

The Strength To Forgive

Catharine could not have imagined the next test of her strength. In July 1870, someone knocked on her door and told her that her son, Harry, had been murdered by convicts who were escaping from Kingston prison.

Looking for crumbs of comfort, Catharine wrote to Frances, saying at least "For him there is no care or pain or trial of earthly grief. No evil messenger knocks on his door with tidings of mishap."

She wrote to Harry's wife, Lily, left in poverty with three children and offered to take in their little daughter, the only way she could help.

So the Lakefield house became full of Katies; Catharine herself, 68; her oldest daughter, known as Aunt Kate, 34; and Little Katie, 3.

Despite her grief, Catharine wrote to and visited the mother of the man who had killed her son. He would be hung for his crime, but Catharine said she would pray for his soul and forgive him.

It was a proper Christian thing to do, but as her sister Susanna wrote, it took great "moral courage".

A skating party at Rideau Hall

Her Greatest Work

Catharine courageously carried on. Now in her seventies, she often caught chest colds, and her arthritis made it hard to walk or hold a pen.

However, she had many letters to answer in between visits to people who needed her. She was becoming steadily famous, and science experts in many fields wrote to her.

John Macoun, an old Scottish friend and now Canada's chief botanist, asked her to review his huge *Catalogue of Canadian Plants*.

Sandford Fleming discussed ideas with her. A railroad surveyor and engineer who invented time zones, he had been a friend since his youth in Peterborough.

James Fletcher, a librarian at the Parliament buildings, an entomologist and botanist, liked Catharine and her work so much that he helped her revise and get *Studies of Plant Life in Canada: or Gleanings From Forest, Lake and Plain* into print in 1885. It was nearly three hundred large, detailed pages, with ten new lithograph illustrations by Agnes.

To get paid, she had to sell copies herself, but finally, the work she cared most about was available for all to read.

FAME IN THE CAPITAL

Catharine visited Ottawa. She met her scientist friends and was invited to Rideau Hall by the Governor General for an evening outdoor gathering, with a bonfire, an ice rink and a toboggan hill.

Catharine, eighty-two, used to rough chinked log houses, was amused by the wood panelled "log cabin" that served as a tea-room. It would have been a palace to an early settler.

She found all the fuss absurd when she was pointed out as the "famous Mrs. Traill". Always practical, she noted "It is good for the book—some will get copies out of curiosity now."

Kate Traill

TINY WILDERNESS

When Catharine heard that Polly Cow's Island had been promised to her, she wrote to Willie that she "ought to be a happy as a Queen with a little kingdom to reign over."

Polly Cow's Island is in Lake Katchewanooka near the entrance to the Burleigh Falls locks, on the Trent-Severn canal. It is only about two hundred square metres of rock, but full of trees and shrubs and Catharine's favourite ferns, mosses and lichens.

Lake Katchewanooka

"Daring Old Lady"

Catharine liked the title "Old Naturalist". She was both. She often signed her letters as "old mother" or introduced herself as "the aged authoress". But even in her nineties, she was no shy violet.

One year, Catharine and her daughter came home from holidaying at Kate's cottage on Stoney Lake. They found surveyors on Westove property, planning to run railroad tracks between the garden and the lake. Catharine stomped out with her stick to protest to the surprised boss. She got the track rerouted.

The "aged authoress" wrote to Sir Sandford Fleming when she heard that two islands she loved in Lake Katchewanooka might be built upon. They were a fragile habitat with endangered species. One was also believed to have an Indian grave she felt should remain undisturbed.

She boldly suggested he use his influence to get them given to her for "literary services to Canada".

He did and though she had to buy one of the islands, in 1893 she was thrilled to receive Polly Cow Island as a gift.

BEARING FRUIT

When Catharine's first grandson was two and a half, he planted seeds from an apple grown in Westove's garden. He watched them sprout and toddled after her, taking care of the little saplings. He died at four of scarlet fever. Nine years later, Catharine wrote to Annie, his mother, that "your darling Harry's apple tree is full of beautiful apples—very fine cooking apples, the first it has ever borne." She promised to lay some by for Annie and suggested that his remaining brothers and sisters plant the pips from those apples in their own gardens.

Longevity

Catharine's long life meant she outlived all her brothers and sisters and many of her friends.

Susanna was ill before she died with a form of dementia at age eighty-two, her fine mind and memory destroyed, though she had odd moments of remembering their childhood. Catharine stayed with her, soothed her by playing hymns on the piano and was with her at the end. At the time, she saw Susanna's death as a merciful release, but later Catharine wrote of her genius and how much she missed her.

Her earliest Canadian friend, Frances Stewart, died in 1872, when Catharine was seventy.

Westove became a family refuge in times of trouble. In her nineties, Catharine was still helping to nurse the needy ones. Her daughter Mary and two adult grandchildren stayed with her till their deaths.

But also to Westove came visitors who were full of life. Catharine's smiles deepened the wrinkles in her face as Willie's son, in from the northwest, leaned down to kiss her. She welcomed grandnieces, grandnephews and even the grandchildren of her friends, delighted to meet in person those she knew only by letter.

Catharine, far left, on the porch, 1899

Ambition Achieved

While naturally interested in any reviews of her work, Catharine most enjoyed being interviewed by a schoolchild who had read *Pearls and Pebbles* and *Cot and Cradle Stories,* a similar volume published by Caswell in 1895. He critiqued them in detail for her, saying the second book was better than the first. She wrote to Anne: "The child's approval was more to me than all the writers in the newspapers for it was genuine."

Besides letters, Catharine was writing the Strickland family story, and her own biography, *Under the Pines.* Neither were published, but Catharine still had literary success to come.

Agnes's daughter Maime, who as a child helped colour the *Wildflowers* book, bicycled to Lakefield one day with a friend named Edward Caswell, an editor.

Catharine was pleased he was interested in a collection of short essays about Canadian nature. It was a long time since she had published anything for young readers, yet that was where she had begun as an author. She asked Maime to help her rewrite them. Catharine's eighty-six year old memory found it hard work. She joked, "Indeed I have well nigh worn out the old brains."

Pearls and Pebbles, or Notes of an Old Naturalist, came out in 1894. It was immediately popular. Catharine had answered the Canadian public's need for this kind of literature. One important reviewer said it was like Gilbert White's book about Selborne. Since her earliest writing years, Catharine had wished to emulate that book, a classic of its kind. At last, she had succeeded.

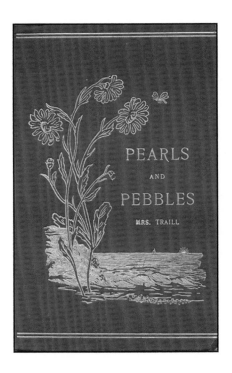

Ups and Downs

FERN COLLECTION

Catharine grew twenty-three different kinds of native Ontario ferns in her garden. In her notebook, she had a list of ten more "not yet under cultivation" that she was hoping to include one day.

She always wrote their proper botanical name, in Latin, but many of them had descriptive common names, for example: Ostrich feather fern, Interrupted fern, Sensitive fern, Creeping bladder fern and Hairy or Maidenhair fern.

She was honoured by having a fern named after her, Mrs. Traill's Shield Fern, Aspidium marginale var. Traillae.

Catharine's life continued to be full of contrasts. The year she was ninety-four is a good example.

She was named an honorary member of the Canadian Women's Historical Society of Toronto, and also Honorary President of the Peterborough Historical Society. She went to the Peterborough meeting. Her deafness made it hard to hear the speeches, but she was pleased, "all the better—that I am not obliged to do or say or write anything—beyond my name in a big book..."

Catharine enjoyed buying a doll to send to her great-grandchildren out west, but she sorrowed for her granddaughter who was suffering and dying at Westove.

She pottered about, leaning on her cherrywood staff, gathering ferns for the garden when she herself was well and hoped for more sales for *Cot and Cradle Stories*, her latest children's book. Then this famous old lady found out that the investment company she had put her money in was bankrupt.

Once more Catharine faced dire poverty.

Funds From Friends All Over

Sir Sandford Fleming

A TOKEN OF ESTEEM

In his letter asking for contributions, Sir Sandford Fleming reminded people that "Mrs. Traill...has rendered service of no ordinary kind in making known the advantages offered by Canada as a field for settlement."

He wrote to Catharine: "You have been instrumental, under Divine Providence, in leading many to love the treasures of Nature, and to read the lessons that are patent in the beauty, symmetry and grace which you have so faithfully portrayed in the flora and Fauna of our woods and forests...we cannot forget the courage with which you endured...we desire to pay tribute to your personal worth."

Catharine had faith that things would work out, but she had to try to help herself too. She asked the Royal Literary Fund for money, since she received nothing from the many copies of her books out in Britain. She tried to think of new work, but just couldn't concentrate. Her hand was too shaky to write and her eyes too tired.

Others wanted to help. Catharine's great-granddaughter wrote to the British Prime Minister and told him about Catharine, the oldest living author in the British Empire. He promised a grant of £150, if money was raised in Canada.

A Testimonial Fund was set up by Sandford Fleming, now Sir Sandford. Many prominent people contributed to it; politicians, such as the Governor General; Canada's leading scientists, lawyers and businessmen. They surprised Catharine with more than £1000.

Catharine was very grateful. "In what words dearest Friend shall I thank you, and all my known and unknown friends in England and Ontario. I can only adopt the hearty simple phrase used by the Indian women— 'I bless you in my heart' ".

Last Days

Her money worries over, Catharine sat on the porch, sewing patchwork quilts, watching the birds. She began yet another book, *Mrs. Margery Pie's History of the Birds of Canada*. She wrote letters to Emma Hubbard, who was helping her publish.

She had weeks of pain and illness, but on a good day, she would dress herself and leave her room. She never liked being cooped up inside. "I long for air and pottering about the garden and the sight of green things is life to me."

At Minnewawa, Kate would settle her on cushions among the grasses and shrubs beneath the pines. "Lots of flowers and berries made me quite happy" she wrote to granddaughter Katie, telling her about the eleven people who came for supper, and apologizing for not writing before as promised.

When Kate brought her back to Westove, Catharine began her last letter, consoling Emma for not finding a publisher yet. She well knew that problem!

She died peacefully in her bed August 29, 1899, aged ninety-seven.

WHAT'S IN A NAME?

A magpie is an English bird like a crow, but with dramatic black, white and iridescent green feathers. It loves to collect treasures such as shiny stones, paper, glass or metal and spend time arranging them. Perhaps Mrs. Margery Pie is Catharine's name for herself, a lifelong collector of natural treasures, which she arranged in her writings.

Catharine's gravestone in Hillside Cemetery, Lakefield

Typical Catharine
All In One Letter

This is part of a letter to Ellen Stewart Dunlop, written one Friday in July 1889. Catharine was eighty-seven. It describes a day when her nephew, George Strickland, took her to Eagle Mount to see where he and his partner were quarrying granite for buildings in Toronto.

"Mr. Frazer gave me a cube of the stone to take home—pretty heavy it is. He says it will take a fine polish... There are buildings putting up and a spacious wharf for loading the vessels—great flat boats. What an undertaking this mining or quarrying rather seems and, yet the work seems to present no difficulties if one may judge by the piles of cut stone...it cleaves so clean and sharp, with a peck and a blow, at once.

I looked up to the lofty height of the great mass and marvelled as I looked at Nature's own masonry—built tier above tier. I noticed the lovely mosses and hair-bells that take root in the crevices of the hard rock find food even in the very hardest spots. Is it not like our own hearts?

Now I must not go on with these subjects though so suggestive of other higher thoughts for I have to get my peas and shell them and the potatoes for Dinner and the time is running on to noon so must soon lay down my pen."

After she says she must not go on, she writes eight more sentences, sending love to all Ellen's dear ones!

She signed it: "Sincerely attached old friend CP Traill".

Legacy

Catharine Parr Traill left a large written legacy, but always wanted to do more.

"...night comes before I am aware how time goes by...how much is left undone that should have been done—and how much forgotten that should have been remembered—I often mourn over the Omissions of my life—I think they tell more heavily on us than the wilful sins..."

She wrote in her last letter: "I never see anything good in my writings till they are in print and even then I wonder how that event came to pass."

What a confession for a best-selling, longest living author!

Her stories for children, the writing she most enjoyed, showed the delight she found, even in the most difficult times of her life. Her guides for settlers were practical and encouraging. Her studies of plants and birds were a record of beauty and change. Her loving descriptions of the wilderness began a long tradition of the place of nature in Canadian stories. Even today, Catharine Parr Traill's name and her dedicated spirit are invoked in Canada's literature.

Catharine's Published Works

The Tell Tale: An Original Collection of Moral and Amusing Stories (London: Harris, 1818)

Disobedience; or Mind What Mama Says

Reformation; or The Cousins (London: James Woodhouse 1819)

Nursery Fables (London: Harris 1821)

Little Downy; or, The History of A Field Mouse: A Moral Tale (London: Dean and Munday 1822)

The Flower Basket; or Poetical Blossoms: Original Nursery Rhymes and Tales (London: A.K. Newman, 1825)

Prejudice Reproved; or, The History of the Negro Toy-Seller (London: Harvey and Darton, 1826)

The Young Emigrants; or Pictures of life in Canada, Calculated to Amuse and Instruct the Minds of Youth (London: Harvey and Darton, 1826)

The Juvenile Forget-Me-Not; or Cabinet of Entertainment and Instruction with other Stricklands (London: N. Hailes, 1827)

Contributions to English annuals for children, often unattributed, 1827-31

The Keepsake Guineas; or, The Best Use of Money (London: A.K. Newman 1828)

Amendment; or Charles Grant and His Sister (London: Dean and Munday, 1828)

The Stepbrothers: A Tale (London: Harvey and Darton, 1828)

Sketches From Nature; or Hints to Juvenile Naturalists (London: Harvey and Darton, 1830)

Sketchbook of a Young Naturalist; or, Hints to the Students of Nature (London: Harvey and Darton, 1831)

Narratives of Nature

History Book for Young Naturalists (London: Edward Lacey, 1831)

The Backwoods of Canada (London: Charles Knight, 1836)

"The Mill of the Rapids: A Canadian Sketch" "Canadian Lumberers" in *Chambers's Edinburgh Journal*, 1838

"The Lost Child" in *Chambers Edinburgh Journal*, 1839

pieces for *Literary Garland*, (Montreal: John Lovell, 1840)

"A Canadian Scene" in *Chambers's Edinburgh Journal*, 1843

"The Settlers Settled; or Pat Connor and His Two Masters" in *Sharpe's London Journal*, 1849

"The Interrupted Bridal: A True Story of the First Rebellion in the Colony"

"The Two Widows of Hunter's Creek"

"The Canadian Emigrant's Farewell" in *The Home Circle*, 1849

Canadian Crusoes: A Tale of the Rice Lake Plains (London: Hall, Virtue, 1852)

"Forest Gleanings" a series of 13 sketches on backwoods life and the Rice Lake Plains in *Anglo-American Magazine*, 1852-3

"The Governor's Daughter " appears in 12 monthly installments in *Maple Leaf*, Toronto, 1853

The Female Emigrant's Guide, and Hints on Canadian Housekeeping (Toronto: Maclear, 1854)

Lady Mary and Her Nurse; or a Peep into the Canadian Forest (London: Hall, Virtue, 1856)

Canadian Wildflowers (Montreal: John Lovell, 1867)

Studies of Plant Life in Canada; or Gleanings from Forest, Lake and Plain (Ottawa: A.S. Woodburn, 1885)

Pearls and Pebbles; or Notes of an Old Naturalist (Toronto:William Briggs, 1894)

Cot and Cradle Stories (Toronto: William Briggs, 1895)

Catharine's life and times

1802	January 9, Catharine is born in England.
1803-1817	Growing up in the countryside.
1818	Death of Catharine's father. First story published at age 16.
1819-1832	Steady career, published many children's books, e.g. Nursery Tales, *Little Downy the Field Mouse, Sketchbook of a Young Naturalist* etc.
1825	Brother Samuel, 20, goes to Canada.
1830	Engagement to Francis Harral at age 28.
1831	Ends engagement to Francis Harral. Sister Susanna marries John Moodie.
1832	Birth of first niece in February. Marries Thomas Traill on May 13. Sails for Canada early July. Arrives Montreal late August. Survives cholera. Moves to Peterborough area. Meets Frances Stewart.
1833	Birth of first son, James George, June 7. Moves into first home, Westove, Douro, December 11.
1836	*The Backwoods of Canada: Being Letters from the Wife of an Emigrant Officer, Illustrative of the Domestic Economy of British America* published. Birth of second child, first daughter, Katherine Agnes (Kate), March 8. Catharine is 34.
1837	Birth of third child, second son, Thomas Henry (Harry), May 16. Rebellion in Upper Canada, husband goes to fight rebels.
1838	Scottish magazine publishes Canadian short stories. Birth of fourth child, second daughter, Anne, Dec. 14. Debts mounting.
1839	Sale of Westove, Douro, move to Ashburnham Village. More short stories.
1840	Birth of fifth child, third daughter, Mary Helen, October 30. Canadian magazines publish stories.
1841	Death of daughter Mary Helen. Birth of sixth child, fourth daughter, Mary Elizabeth Jane, November 7.
1842	Birth of seventh child, fifth daughter, Eleanor Stewart, baptized July 11. Death of Eleanor, buried Oct. 14. Catharine is 40.
1843	Moves to "Saville Farm".

1844	Birth of eighth child, third son, William Edward, July 26
1845-7	Moves to Ashburnham Village, Wolf Tower, and Mt. Ararat.
1848	Birth of ninth child, fourth son, Walter John, August 9.
1849	Moves to "Oaklands" farm, Rice Lake Plain near Gore's Landing. More short pieces in British magazines.
1852	*The Canadian Crusoes: A Tale of the Rice Lake Plains* published at age 50.
1853-6	*The Governor's Daughter* published in installments, *The Female Emigrant's Guide, Lady Mary and Her Nurse,* published. James marries.
1857	House burns down. Lives with friends and relatives. Anne marries. Birth of first grandchild, son of James.
1859	Illness and death of husband, Thomas Traill, June 21.
1860	Lives in Lakefield, builds second Westove.
1861-6	Mary marries. Henry marries. Death of mother in England. William and Walter go west.
1867	Death of brother, Sam, Jan. 11. Death of son, James, April 14. Catharine is 65.
1868	*Canadian Wildflowers* published. William marries.
1870	Death of son Harry, adoption of granddaughter. July 7.
1872	Death of Frances Stewart, Feb. 24.
1874-84	Deaths of two sisters and brother in England, Walter marries. Catharine is honoured at Rideau Hall.
1885	*Studies of Plant Life in Canada; or Gleanings from Forest, Lake and Plain* published. Death of Susanna, April 8.
1886-96	Deaths of remaining two sisters in England. Death of daughter Mary and her two grown children. Honoured by gift of Polly Cow Island. *Pearls and Pebbles: Tales of An Old Naturalist* and *Cot and Cradle Stories* published. Made honorary president of Peterborough Historical Society, and honorary member of Canadian Women's Historical Society.
1897	At age 95, receives Testimonial Fund led by Sir Sandford Fleming.
1899	Catharine dies, August 29, aged ninety-seven.

About the Author

Lynn Westerhout immigrated to Canada from England as a child. She spent her teenage years in and around Montreal, then moved to Toronto. Lynn is the winner of the Frances E. Russell Award for her work on *Making It Home*. Her other works include picture books called *Business in Bangkok* and *Baggage To London*.

Lynn does storytelling programs for young audiences. She is also a founding teaching staff member of Centauri Adult Arts Retreat and she teaches creative writing for adults for the Toronto Board of Education. Her interests run, in no particular order of priority, to reading, banjo playing, reading, morris dancing, singing, reading, crafts, gardening and reading anything and everything. She is the mother of three and a grandmother. She lives in Toronto with her husband and a springer spaniel.

Acknowledgements

First to Sydell Waxman and Sylvia McConnell, who gave me the chance to do this book.

However, it could not have been accomplished without the work of the historians who wrote the resources to which I turned. To be able to read letters and journal entries from Catharine, without having to "puzzle out" her handwriting, as her sister Agnes once complained, was a great boon. To have the insights and sources suggested by other writers of the history of Ontario pioneer times and the Strickland family was also most helpful. I thank the committee of the Frances E. Russell award for making it easier for me to take advantage of those resources. Thanks also to the volunteers of the Christ Church, North Douro museum, and the friendly people of Lakefield. Thank you, Mike J. Shchepanek, Chief Collection Manager of the Botany section of the Canadian Museum of Nature for answering my questions about Catharine's hated fireweed.

I thank my husband Tam Kearney for his patience and companionship on my travels to places in Catharine's life, and his sister and brother-in-law, Helen and Gordon Turnbull, for the surprise chance to visit Norfolk and Suffolk, while we visited with them in Scotland. I thank my writing group, Sydell Waxman, Rona Arato and Frieda Wishinsky, for their continued support and commentary and very special thanks go to my sister, Lisa Westerhout, who stayed up all night during a rare visit, reading and editing. I am a very lucky writer.

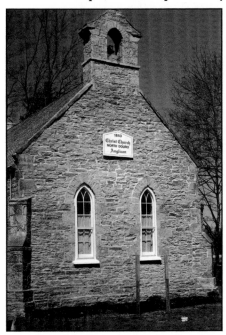

Christ Church in Lakefield, Ontario, which now houses a museum about Catharine and other writers of the town such as Isabella Valancy Crawford and Margaret Laurence.

A few of the books that were used while researching this story

All of Catharine's works plus her family's.

I Bless You In My Heart: Selected Correspondence of Catharine Parr Traill edited by Carl Ballstadt, Elizabeth Hopkins and Michael A. Peterman (Toronto: University of Toronto Press, 1996)

Lady of the Backwoods by Sara Eaton (Toronto: McClelland and Stewart, 1969)

Sisters in the Wilderness: The Lives of Susanna Moodie and Catharine Parr Traill by Charlotte Gray (Toronto: Penguin Books Canada, 1999)

Catharine Parr Traill and Her Works by Carl Ballstadt (Downsview: ECW Press, 1983)

Gentle Pioneers: Five Nineteenth-Century Canadians by Audrey Y. Morris (Toronto and London: Hodder and Stoughton 1968)

Nelson's Falls to Lakefield: A History of the Village by Bob Delledonne (Lakefield, Ontario, Canada, Lakefield Historical Society, 1999)

"My Old Friend the Otonabee": Glimpses by Samuel Strickland, Catharine Parr Traill & Susanna Moodie by Michael Peterman (Peterborough, Ontario, Canada: Peterborough Historical Society 1999)

Through the Years In Douro, Peterborough County, Canada 1822-1967 edited by J. Alex Edmison, Q.C. (Peterborough, Ontario, Canada: A.D. Newson Co. 1967, third revised edition 1978)

House Calls: The True Story of a Pioneer Doctor by Ainslie Manson, illustrated by Mary Jane Gerber (Toronto: Groundwood Books 2001)

From Douro to Dublin: The Letters of Frances Stewart by Joyce C. Lewis (Peterborough: Peterborough Historical Society, occasional paper 14, 1994)

Sandford Fleming: No Better Inheritance by Jean Murray Cole (Peterborough: Peterborough Historical Society, occasional paper 11, Nov. 1990)

Peterborough in the Hutchison-Fleming Era 1845-1846 by Jean Murray Cole (Peterborough: Peterborough Historical Society, occasional paper 5, Sept. 1984

Kingston Penitentiary: The First Hundred and Fifty Years 1835-1985 by Dennis Curtis and others (The Correctional Service of Canada, Ottawa, 1985)

Index of quotes used in this book

65	"I no longer -death"	Letter to Frances Stewart, #48 in *I Bless You* p.171
65	"was -ever saw!"	Letter to Frances Stewart, #48 in *I Bless You* p.172
66	"beautiful -Canada"	Montreal Daily News quoted in *Sisters in the Wilderness* p.299
67	"staring, winking and laughing"	*Kingston Penitentiary 1835-1985* p.43
67	"For him-mishap"	Letter to Frances Stewart, #53 in *I Bless You* p.185
67	"moral courage."	Susanna to Allen Ransome, #111 in *Letters of a Lifetime* ` p.299
68	"It is good-curiosity now."	Letter to Ellen Dunlop, #72 in *I Bless You* p.238
69	"literary services -Canada"	Letter to William Traill, #108 in *I Bless You* p.356
69	"ought be -reign over."	Letter to William Traill, #108 in *I Bless You* p.356
70	"your darling -borne"	Letter to Annie Atwood, #59 in *I Bless You* p.201
71	"Indeed -brains."	Letter to William Traill, #91, in *I Bless You* p.312
71	"The child's -genuine."	Letter to Annie Atwood, #123 in *I Bless You* p.382
72	"all the -big book"	Letter to Annie Atwood, #123 in *I Bless You* p.381
72	"not yet -cultivation"	Catharine's notes, Traill Family Coll. 3960 NAC
73	"Mrs. Traill -settlement"	Sir Sandford Fleming, in *Sisters in the Wilderness* p.345
73	"You have been -worth."	Tribute with Testimonial Fund, in *I Bless You* p.270
73	"In what -heart."	Letter to Sir Sandford Fleming, #129 in *I Bless You* p.392
74	"I long -life to me."	Letter to Annie Atwood, #89, in *I Bless You* p.308
74	"Lots of flowers -happy."	Letter to Katie Traill, #134 in *I Bless You* p.398
75	"Mr. Frazer -my pen	Letter to Ellen Dunlop, #95 in *I Bless You* p.322
76	"night comes -wilful sins"	Letter to Rob't & Caro Strickland, #96 in *I Bless You* p.323
76	"I never-pass."	Letter to Emma Hubbard, #136 in *I Bless You* p.401

Index and Glossary of Who's Who and What's What

Photo and Art Credits